Electronically Recorded Evidence

Fourmat Publishing

Electronically Recorded Evidence

A guide to the use of tape and video recordings in criminal and civil proceedings

by Sybil Sharpe, Barrister

London
Fourmat Publishing
1989

ISBN 1 85190 071 3

First published 1989

Published by Fourmat Publishing, 27 & 28 St Albans Place,
Islington Green, London N1 ONX
Typeset by Pentacor Ltd, High Wycombe
Printed in Great Britain by
Billing & Sons Ltd, Worcester

Preface

The extent to which the courts admit electronically recorded evidence underlines the current and increasing use of new technology in the judicial process. Information has been recorded over the centuries by a variety of methods: "the common case once was that it was not on paper but on parchment; and long before that it was on stone, marble, or clay" (*Rex* v *Daye*, 1908). The courts have always taken a pragmatic approach to the evolution of new rules to deal with new situations. Today, in an increasingly technological society, electronically recorded evidence is replacing the notebook and the testimony of eye witnesses as a method of proof.

The use made of video and tape recorded evidence is now so frequent that it is necessary for all those involved with the civil and criminal process to be aware of the issues that arise therefrom (for instance, in relation to identification evidence and admissions). Those who use such recordings in a professional capacity, such as journalists and social workers, should be aware of the litigious purposes to which their recordings may be put and the extent to which they may be compelled to disclose such recordings in litigation. Over the last two years a body of case law has developed surrounding these issues, and statute has provided for the reception of evidence by television link in certain cases. A code governing the conduct of tape recorded interviews with suspects has finally been laid before Parliament. This volume makes reference, *inter alia*, to recent case law on electronically recorded evidence, the code of conduct on the tape recording of interviews made pursuant to Police and Criminal Evidence Act and to the new Crown Court rules for interviewing children by means of closed circuit television link. The evidential provisions of the Criminal Justice Act 1988 are discussed in the context of electronically recorded evidence generally and in relation to child witnesses in particular.

My thanks are due to the officers of the West Midlands Police force (in particular Detective Superintendent Beechey and Inspector Mackie) for giving me their time and the benefit of their experience.

Sybil Sharpe
February 1989

Contents

Table of cases

Chapter 1

Video or tape recordings as original evidence

1. Introduction

The 1960s saw the advent of audio recordings as evidence in court proceedings. In the 1980s both audio and video recordings are increasingly taking the place of eye witness testimony. The advantages of the new forms of evidence are obvious. In many cases the subject of the recording is unaware that he is being observed; the evidence may be more reliable than testimony; and the court can form an opinion as to the weight to be attached to the out-of-court evidence, having viewed it in court. Such electronically produced proof is still governed by the law of evidence, however.

This chapter is concerned with the situations in which such recordings may be used to present evidence, and with the issues that arise when such evidence is treated as original evidence. Where the tape is tendered *as original evidence*, it is adduced to show simply that it exists; and not as evidence of truth of any matter contained in the tape. Thus a recording made of a conversation between two accused at a police station is original evidence if tendered to prove that the conversation took place, rather than to prove the truth of what was said in that conversation. If a recording is adduced in evidence to prove the truth of the matter recorded therein (for example, that statements made in the course of a police interview were in fact true) the recording is hearsay rather than original evidence and as such may become documentary evidence (see Chapter 2).

Evidence obtained through electronic recording devices is admissible on the same principles as eye witness testimony. This was established in *R* v *Grimer* (1982) where it was stated that there was no distinction between the evidence of a man who looked at a video tape (provided there was no challenge to the validity of the tape itself) from that of a bystander who observed the primary facts. Thus a witness may testify that he made an out of court identification before trial on the basis of seeing a video recording or a section of news film shown on television in exactly the same way as he could testify to an identification made with his naked eye on seeing the accused committing the crime. The identification based upon the recorded evidence has the obvious advantage that it can be made some time subsequent to the commission of the alleged offence. In *Grimer* a security officer viewed a tape recording of a theft from shop premises and was able to testify as to identification of the offender on the basis of the recording (which was also viewed by the court). In *Kajala* v *Noble* (1982) a witness identified the accused from a television news bulletin and was able to testify in court that he had made this identification. Issues of admissibility are dealt with in detail at page 9 below.

There is no distinction between one form of recorded evidence and another. In *R* v *Fowden and White* (1982) it was stated that there was no difference in principle between a video film and a photograph or a tape recording. See also *R* v *Maqsud Ali* (1966) where it was emphasised that the accuracy of the recording had to be proved and the recorded voices properly identified.

2. Situations where recorded evidence may be presented in court

(a) To prove the commission of a crime

Where it is anticipated that a crime may be committed, the electronic "eyes" and "ears" of microphones and cameras will perform a surveillance function and provide evidence against the perpetrator. In *R* v *McShane* (1977), secretly made video and sound recordings of a conversation between mother and daughter were adduced to prove a charge of attempting to counsel or procure a suicide. The daughter was seen to pin a packet of Nembutal tablets inside her mother's clothing and was heard to tell her mother the number of tablets it was necessary to take. The recordings were available to the jury at trial. Also, in *R* v *Jordan* (1981) a microphone and a concealed single fixed video camera were used to record an alleged "knock out" held by dealers at the conclusion of an auction. In both cases the recordings were admissible in court to prove that a crime had actually been committed in circumstances that might equally have been consistent with innocent association. In both cases the identity of the offenders was known and the issue was one of whether a criminal activity had taken place. The quality of the evidence produced in *Jordan* was so unsatisfactory, however, that it had to be supported by the testimony of police officers who had passed in and out of the hotel room purporting to be hotel staff.

(b) To identify the perpetrators of a crime

This is by far the commonest use currently made of electronically recorded evidence. Traditionally, such recordings have been made in premises such as banks and shops as an adjunct to or in substitution for the store detective or security officer. Both *Grimer* and *Fowden and White* (above) were shoplifting cases, but recording equipment is now being used at football grounds (to identify public disorder offenders); on the top decks of some public transport vehicles; and by motorway patrols. On 20 January 1988 *The Times* reproduced three photographs taken by closed circuit television at a football ground, together with the headline "How the cameras caught the hooligan in the act". The paper reported that the offender was spotted by neither policemen nor club stewards. He pleaded guilty, having been told that his action was caught perfectly on film. If he had not done so, the film would have been admissible at trial to prove both identity and criminal activity.

In July 1988, a British court received video film evidence of a motoring offence for the first time, when a recording was submitted to Solihull magistrates. The recording had been made from the dashboard of an unmarked police car. The defendant admitted driving without due care and attention.

It is clearly more likely that the accused will plead guilty if his identity and his actions are recorded on film. However, in March 1988, Michael Groce was acquitted of robbery after the jury rejected identification evidence based on a colour video film of the event at a building society. The camera was pointing at the door of the premises. No pictures of the hold-up at the counter were available, but two men were recorded loitering outside the premises and then entering. It was alleged that Mr Groce was one of those two men. This was denied by the accused. The jury was shown another film of Mr Groce walking in a London street. Mr Groce did not deny that the second film was a recording of him. A comparison was made with the building society film. The jury rejected an argument, based upon computer analysis of similarities between the two films, that the man depicted in both films was the same person.

Further, in March 1989, "digital enhancement" of a video film of a bank raid led experts to conclude that it was "highly probable" that the appellant (Ernest Barrie) was not the man on film, despite eye-witness identification.

(c) To provide evidence of the scene of a crime

A video recording can be admitted as evidence of the scene of the crime in preference to maps, plans or still photographs. In *R* v *Thomas* (1986), a videotape of the scene of a car chase was admitted in evidence by agreement in order that a police officer could tie up his notes with a visual presentation. It was stated that it was desirable that the recording should be made as soon as possible after the event and that the conditions existing at the time, such as road repairs and overgrown hedgerows, should be present on the video recording. It is to be noted that although this evidence is essentially a reconstruction, it may none the less be admissible.

(d) To provide a confession by means of re-enactment

The only authority to support this use of video recording is the Privy Council case of *Li Shu-Ling* v *The Queen* (1988). The appellant's defence to a murder charge was that he accidentally strangled his victim whilst attempting to stop her screaming after a quarrel. The appellant had made a full confession, and was asked if he would be willing to re-enact the scene, being reminded that he was still under caution and that he was not obliged to agree to the re-enactment. He expressed his willingness to participate and knew that the re-enactment would be recorded on video tape. A woman detective inspector played the part of the victim. The appellant also gave a running commentary explaining his movements. The trial judge admitted the re-enactment as a visual confirmation of the earlier oral confession. On appeal to the Privy Council, it was held that the recording was admissible. Lord Griffiths stated:

> "If it was permissible to allow an accused to re-enact a part of the crime during interrogation there was no reason in principle why, if he was prepared to do so, he should not show how he committed the crime at the scene of the crime."

At present the re-enactment of grave offences is established in Hong Kong, Australia and the United States. Such a practice was given the cautious approval of the Court, provided that the accused was given a proper warning that he need not take part and provided that the film was shown to the accused as soon as practicable after it had been completed so that he could make a contemporaneous recording of any comments or criticisms. It is more difficult for the accused to escape from the consequences of such a demonstration than to challenge an oral confession which he could allege contained a misunderstanding.

For a fuller discussion of recorded reconstructions, see page 9 *et seq*.

(e) To show the process of identification

A video recording may be made of an identification parade or group identification, although recording is only mandatory under the Codes of Practice under the Police and Criminal Evidence Act 1984 ("PACE") when identification takes place in a room containing a one way screen (enabling the witness to see members of the parade or to see the suspect in a confrontation without being seen), and the suspect has no solicitor, friend or appropriate adult present.

In *R* v *Smith and Doe* (1987) an elderly witness identified the second defendant at a group identification which took place in a shopping precinct (both defendants were brought down an escalator at the precinct). The defendants had been charged with burglary of a dwelling house and the case rested to a large extent upon identification evidence. At the full committal hearing, the witness had difficulty in distinguishing between the defendants. Before the trial, she was shown a videotape of the events in the precinct.

The defence objected to the admissibility of the tape and to the evidence of the police officer as to what happened when the witness watched the tape. Although the appellants' appeal was allowed in these particular circumstances (the recorded evidence was tendered to bolster the weak identification evidence of the witness and this was not permissible), it was stated that a film of the process of identification can have legitimate uses, for example to inform the jury of the difficulty or ease with which a witness identifies a suspect. A video recording can clearly be used to establish the credibility of an identification made by a witness where that witness testifies in court to the previous identification. Where a witness fails to confirm the previous out-of-court identification, and fails to make an in-court identification of the suspect, the video tape may perhaps be admitted as documentary evidence (see Chapter 2). If the recording is so admitted, it may be substituted for the testimony of a witness, thus avoiding the problems of hearsay evidence that arose in *R* v *Osbourne and Virtue* (1973). There, a police officer's testimony that he had seen the witness identify Osbourne at a parade was admitted, even though the witness had no memory of so doing and could not identify Osbourne at the trial.

(f) To provide evidence of police interviews

Where a police officer's written record of a tape recorded interview is not accepted by the defence, the master tape becomes an exhibit in court proceedings (see Chapter 6).

3. Closed circuit television links

Video links do not amount to *recorded* evidence. They are "live", and recorded evidence is by definition not live, having been made in advance of trial. None the less, it is convenient to mention the use of video links at this stage. Further, a film of evidence given by means of closed circuit television (if adduced on appeal) would clearly be recorded evidence. In these situations, the witness takes a full part in the proceedings, but is not physically present in the court room. The witness may be examined and cross-examined in the usual way and his response and demeanour will be visible on screen in court.

Section 32 of the Criminal Justice Act 1988 came into force on 5 January 1989, except for the provisions concerning witnesses outside the UK, which are likely to be in force in July 1989. The section makes provision for the use of closed circuit television links in trials on indictment, or an appeal to the Criminal Division of the Court of Appeal. The provision applies to persons "other than the accused". Two categories of witnesses are entitled to give evidence on closed circuit television—children in certain circumstances; and overseas witnesses.

The reception of evidence by video link (whether in the case of a child witness or in the case of a witness outside the United Kingdom) is subject to the leave of the court (s 32(1)).

(a) Child witnesses

Evidence may be given by closed circuit television where:

(i) the witness is under the age of fourteen years; and

(ii) the offence charged is a sexual offence or an offence of violence or of cruelty under the Children and Young Persons Act 1933.

The offences are specified in full in s 32(2) of the Act and are as follows:

(i) an offence which involves assault on, or injury or a threat of injury to, a person;

(ii) an offence under s 1 Children and Young Persons Act 1933 (cruelty to persons under sixteen);

(iii) an offence under the Sexual Offences Act 1956, Indecency with Children Act 1960, Sexual Offences

Act 1967, s 54 Criminal Law Act 1977, or the Protection of Children Act 1978; and

(iv) an offence which consists of attempting or conspiring to commit, or of aiding, abetting, counselling, procuring or inciting the commission of, an offence falling within the above categories.

The statutes listed above create, amongst others, the offences of rape; incest (and incitement to commit incest); unlawful sexual intercourse; indecent assault; acts of gross indecency with children under fourteen years; and the taking or distributing of indecent photographs of persons under sixteen years. But the offence need not necessarily be of a sexual nature, and the violence (or threat of it) need not even be directed to a person under the age of fourteen years. However, these may be factors in the exercise of judicial discretion to allow evidence to be given by television link (see Chapter 3).

It is to be noted that in the initial stages of the implementation of this provision, not all Crown Courts are equipped with video link facilities. Two or three in each circuit are so equipped and the need for any extension of facilities is to be assessed over a period of time.

The problems surrounding the interviewing and examination of child witnesses when either video recording or video link is used are discussed in full in Chapter 3. It is important to distinguish the two methods. A closed circuit television link allows counsel to cross-examine from the court room and therefore preserves the orality of trial. The admission of recorded evidence would mean the reception of evidence which had not been subject to such cross-examination, being a pre-recorded out of court interview with the child witness.

A government enquiry has been set up to discuss the use of video recorded evidence following various unsuccessful attempts to provide for its admissibility in proposed amendments to the Criminal Justice Bill.

(b) Witnesses outside the United Kingdom

Section 32 Criminal Justice Act 1988 also allows for the evidence of a witness who is outside the United Kingdom to be given by video link. Any statement so made will be treated for the purposes of the Perjury Act 1911 as having been made in the proceedings in which it is given. One object of this provision is to "induce" witnesses to give evidence without asking them to jeopardise their liberty by returning to the United Kingdom, and it is therefore likely to be used in serious fraud cases. There is no such statutory limitation on its use, however.

4. Admissibility

Some of the problems concerning the admissibility of tape recorded and video recorded evidence are discussed below. In all these cases the evidence is treated by the court as original evidence and no question of hearsay arises. The evidential problems concerning recorded evidence that is regarded as documentary are dealt with in Chapter 2.

(a) The "best evidence" rule

The classic statement of the "best evidence" rule is that the evidence presented to the court should be the best that the nature of the case will allow. It has been argued that the rule can no longer be regarded as a general principle of the law of evidence, since it has been honoured more in its breach than in its observance. However, the rule takes on a renewed significance in the context of recorded evidence. Two main issues arise: the first is the admissibility of reconstructions; the second is the admissibility of copy tapes.

A reconstruction of an incident is clearly not of the same probative value as a contemporaneous recording. It is not always easy, however, to determine whether the court will treat this as going to admissibility rather than to weight. Evidence which is ruled inadmissible cannot be adduced before the court. The judge (or jury if it is a criminal case) will not therefore consider it. Evidence which is admissible may nonetheless be considered to be of little significance by a judge or jury in reaching a decision, that is, little weight may be attached to it even though it is admitted.

Weight is essentially a matter of fact, whereas admissibility is a matter of law and can never, therefore, be for a jury to decide. In *R* v *Quinn and Bloom* (1962) a film was made reconstructing a strip-tease performance that had taken place some three months before. The appellants (who had been charged with keeping a disorderly house) wanted the film to be admitted. It was stated:

> "It is of course true that demonstrations are frequently given by witnesses in the witness box to show what was done at the material time . . . such demonstrations usually take place in the witness box, take place in the presence of the jury, and are intended to illustrate one act. In our view such demonstrations are altogether different in character from a reconstruction of an entire scene, a reconstruction which has been brought into existence in private for the purpose of constituting evidence at trial". (per Ashworth J)

The film was not admitted in evidence as it was considered a "most unsatisfactory" method of proof.

However, in *R* v *Thomas*, the reconstruction of the scene of a car chase was allowed in evidence to establish the route taken by the vehicles, and to convey in a much more accurate and helpful way than could be achieved by the use of maps or still photographs, a picture of the roads involved. The logical distinction between the two cases is that *Quinn* was a reconstruction of events, whereas the tape in *Thomas* was used to establish a continuing state of affairs—the narrow and winding nature of the road in question, but not the alleged act of reckless driving itself. Unfortunately this distinction does not hold good for the case of *Li Shu-ling* v *The Queen* (see page 4). If that decision is considered applicable to the United Kingdom, it may be that reconstructions of alleged offences are admissible, provided that the recording takes place in the presence of prosecution and defendant and the defendant is made aware that he is not under any obligation to take part.

The admissibility of copies of tapes of police interviews is covered by the Code of Practice on tape recording under PACE and this is dealt with in Chapter 6. Copy tapes from other sources, for example journalists and social workers, may be tendered in evidence. In *Kajala* v *Noble* (1982) the question arose whether a video cassette made of an original BBC film could be admitted in evidence, together with the testimony of the assistant editor who made the recording, and the testimony of a witness who was familiar with the appellant and could identify him as the man featuring both in the original television film and in the cassette recording. The BBC did not, as a matter of policy, allow original documents out of its custody. The camera crew who made the original film was on an overseas assignment and thus could not testify that the recording shown in court contained what they saw and recorded at the time of the incident. It was held that:

> "The court was not confined to the best evidence, but could admit all relevant evidence. The goodness or badness of it went to weight and not to admissibility. The old rule was confined to written documents in the strict sense of the term and had no relevance to tapes or films".

Thus a copy tape can be admitted in evidence, although if it cannot be proved by oral testimony to be a true copy, no weight will be attached to it. A tape which is allegedly a fabrication may well be inadmissible under s 78 PACE (see page 14). Dicta in *Maqsud Ali* suggest that issues of truth or falsity may in some cases be considered as matters of admissibility, and this probably survives *Kajala* v *Noble*. In *R* v *Stevenson and Others* (1971) the prosecution sought to tender evidence of tape recordings alleged to be conversations between the defendants and a prosecution witness. The defendants contended that the recordings were fabricated and not originals. The *ratio* turned on the word "original". In view of *Kajala* v *Noble*, it is likely that the issue in future cases will be whether to exclude on the basis of falsity alone.

(b) The "Turnbull Guidelines"

The use of video recordings to identify the perpetrators of crime leads to the reception of eye witness testimony based on such evidence. In *Grimer* and *Fowden and White*, the witnesses viewed video recordings of the alleged thefts prior to the trial and identified the suspects from the tapes. In *Grimer*, the witness testified to this out-of-the-court identification in court. In *Fowden and White* such testimony was held in the particular circumstances of the case to have been improperly admitted (see page 16). The tape can, of course, be shown to the court. None the less, if the issue is one of disputed identity, the need for caution before convicting on such evidence still applies. The guidelines laid down in *R* v *Turnbull* (1977) provide:

1. Whenever the evidence against an accused depends wholly or substantially on the correctness of identification evidence, which the defendant alleges to be mistaken, the judge should warn the jury of the special need for caution before convicting on such evidence.
2. The judge should direct the jury to examine closely the circumstances in which the identification was made, taking account of matters such as the distance from which the observation was made and whether the view of the witness was obscured in any way. [Personal factors such as knowledge of the defendant by the witness become relevant in this context where the court is relying on the testimony of a witness who viewed the tape.]
3. The jury should be warned that mistakes in recognition can sometimes be made and any discrepancies between description and actual appearance should be pointed out to the jury. [Such discrepancies would, of course, be visible from the tape, if it is still in existence].
4. If the quality of the identification evidence is good, the judge may leave the jury to assess its value (provided that an adequate warning has been given about the need for caution).
5. If the judge considers the quality of the identifying evidence to be poor, the case should be withdrawn from the jury unless there is other supporting evidence. The judge should point out to the jury which evidence can be capable of supporting the identification.

Where a video recording exists, the court may make its own judgement as to whether the accused appears on the tape. The situation is clearly more difficult where the tape has been accidentally erased after the initial identification has been made. In *Taylor* v *Chief Constable of Cheshire* (1986) a security officer observed an incident, which lasted for a few seconds only, in which he saw the back view of the alleged offender, who then "glanced" at the camera full face before he walked out of camera range. The observation was made on a television screen linked to a remote control camera and a video recorder which had been switched on. The police officers (who viewed the recording subsequently) identified the defendant as the person depicted on it. The video was then viewed by the defendant's solicitor, who formed the opinion that he could not be sure that it was the defendant who was depicted, and further, that no offence was disclosed by the recording. The recording was kept at the shop premises for safe keeping.

Shortly before the hearing, it was discovered that the tape had been erased by new security officers. The evidence adduced in court was thus the testimony of the police officers as to what they had seen depicted on the video. An argument that this was hearsay evidence was (in line with previous authorities) rejected. It was stated, however, that the weight and reliability of the evidence would depend upon an assessment of all relevant considerations:

> "including the clarity of the recording, its length, and, where identification is in issue, the witness's prior knowledge of the person said to be identified, in accordance with well established principles".

Thus the *Turnbull* criteria clearly apply. Further:

> "where there is a recording, a witness has the opportunity to study again and again what may be a fleeting glimpse of a short incident and that study may affect greatly both his ability to describe what he saw and his confidence in an identification. When the film or recording is shown to the court, his evidence . . . can be assessed in the light of what the court can see. When the film or recording is not available, or is not produced, the court will, and in my view must, hesitate and consider very carefully indeed before finding themselves made sure of guilt upon such evidence." (per Gibson LJ)

None the less, this is a matter of weight, not admissibility, and the court is entitled to convict upon such evidence. Thus, as with the question of best evidence, the matter is one of weight rather than admissibility, subject to any discretion which the court may exercise to exclude it (see s 78 PACE; at (*d*) below).

(c) Opinion evidence

In *R* v *Grimer* the witness, who had known the accused socially for a number of years, was allowed to state in court that in his opinion the accused was the man depicted on tape. In *Fowden and White*, the police officer and store detective witnesses were to be called to testify that in their opinion the accused were the persons depicted on film. In the event, it was held that such evidence should have been excluded under the court's discretion.

Whilst it is unobjectionable for a witness to give evidence that he made a previous out-of-court identification of the accused, this should go only to proving the consistency of the in-court identification: *R* v *Christie* (1914). If the witness goes beyond this and opines on the question of whether the recording is in fact a recording of the accused, in other words if he attempts to affirm the accuracy of the out-of-court identification, he infringes the hearsay rule. Support for this view can be found in *dicta* in *Taylor* v *Chief Constable of Cheshire*:

> "There can be no doubt that a witness cannot be called to give his view upon what he has seen in a recording, or indeed upon what he saw direct, that in his opinion an offence of any sort has been committed. All he can do is to describe what he saw, and matters of inference from the primary facts are for the court."

Thus, unless expert opinion evidence (eg. digital enhancement) is adduced, inferences as to any matter raised by the recording are for the court alone to draw.

(d) Discretion to exclude evidence

Section 78 PACE provides:

> "(1) In any proceedings the court may refuse to allow evidence upon which the prosecution proposes to rely to be given if it appears to the court that, having regard to all the circumstances, including the circumstances in which the evidence was obtained, the admission of the evidence would have such an adverse effect on the fairness of the proceedings that the court ought not to admit it.
>
> (2) Nothing in this section shall prejudice any rule of law requiring a court to exclude evidence."

This section is most often relied upon where there has been a breach of the Codes of Practice under PACE (in relation to detention, questioning, the conduct of an identification etc). It also becomes relevant where it is alleged that evidence has been recorded in such circumstances that its admission would adversely affect a fair trial. In *R* v *H* (1987), the defendant was accused of raping his girlfriend. In an interview under caution, he asserted that intercourse had taken place with the woman's consent. He was released pending further enquiries. The police installed tape recording equipment on the woman's telephone with her consent. She then instigated a series of telephone conversations with the defendant. The court upheld the defence objections to the admissibility of the tape recordings, that they were a trap and as such would have an adverse effect on the fairness of the proceedings. The evidence was excluded and the defendant acquitted.

However, in *Maqsud Ali* the court rejected the defence argument that tape recordings of conversations between the defendants, made without their knowledge, should be excluded. One argument for exclusion was based upon the common law *Judges' Rules* which were held not to apply since the men went to the police station voluntarily and therefore were not in custody. It was stated (per Marshall J):

> "The method of the informer and of the eavesdropper is commonly used in the detection of crime. The only difference here was that a mechanical device was the eavesdropper."

It is possible that the decision on this point is no longer good authority since PACE came into operation. The second argument for exclusion, which also failed, was based on the quality (and therefore reliability) of the recording itself. The recording was overlaid with street and other noises. Much of the conversation was inaudible or undecipherable. Much of the conversation was not transcribed. The judge ruled that what was deciphered should be left for the jury to assess. An argument that a translation of the tape in transcript would be unreliable or misleading was also rejected since the jury was guided by what they heard on the tape and by the detailed cross-examination of the translation experts for both sides. It was stated that:

> "the cases must be rare where the judge is satisfied in undertaking his own investigation into the weight of the evidence which, subject to proper directions to the jury, is really the province of the jury, but the court sees that there can be cases—but they must be rare—where issues of admissibility and weight can underlay each other."

It seems therefore that although the weight to be attached to a recording is normally a matter for the jury, it may be that the quality is so poor that it should be excluded under s 78 because its admission would have an adverse effect on the fairness of the proceedings. In such a situation quality would not simply go to weight, but would determine admissibility.

The admissibility of recorded evidence may also be affected by matters extrinsic to the tape in question. In *Fowden and White* it was held that an identification made by a police officer and a store detective on the basis of a video recording should not have been admitted in evidence by the court. The identifying witnesses knew the accused from a similar shoplifting case a week later. The defence were thus precluded from testing the accuracy of the identification without causing prejudice or embarrassment to the accused. Thus if the recorded evidence introduces matters which are *prima facie* inadmissible, such as the character of the accused, it may still be excluded in the discretion of the court.

(e) Tape recorded confessions

Admissions or confessions which are tape recorded are, of course, subject to the same rules of admissibility as those which are not. A tape is original evidence of the interview and only becomes hearsay when the truth of what is said is in issue. Section 76 PACE still applies. Therefore the prosecution has the burden of proving that the confession was not made under oppression nor in consequence of anything said or done which was likely to render it unreliable. Where the interview is tape recorded, challenge to the admissibility of the confession is likely to be on the basis of breach of the *Code of Practice for the Tape Recording of Interviews* rather than on the basis of oppression or unreliability (see Chapter 6).

Chapter 2

Video or tape recordings as documentary evidence

1. Recording methods

The law is not concerned with *how* the evidence has been recorded. Whether it is recorded manually or as part of an automated process is not relevant to the question of admissibility. It was stated in the 1968 case, *The Statue of Liberty*, that:

> "It would be an absurd distinction that a photograph should be admissible if the camera were operated manually by a photographer, but not if it were operated by a trip or clock mechanism. Again cards from clocking-in machines are frequently admitted in accident cases. The law is bound these days to take cognisance of the fact that mechanical means replace human effort." (per Sir Jocelyn Simon P)

An attempt to distinguish *Maqsud Ali* (1966) (see Chapter 1), on the basis that in this case the police officer set up the recording machine to overhear the conversation and claimed to be able to identify the voices recorded, was rejected. However, although the law is not concerned with the method used to record evidence (whether manual or automatic), a distinction must still be made between a tape that is used purely as a recording device (original evidence) and one that is used to create information (documentary evidence). This chapter outlines the law relating to the admissibility of taped evidence where such evidence is documentary in nature. It is, of course, necessary to decide when electronically recorded evidence is regarded as being documentary in nature.

2. The duality of recorded evidence

Electronically recorded evidence may be admissible either as original or as documentary evidence. In the first instance the tape is real evidence. It is produced as a material object for inspection in court. The court is only concerned to see that a matter has been recorded upon tape. It is not concerned with the truth of the matter recorded. In the second instance, an electronic recorder is used to create information which is adduced as proof of the truth of the subject matter of the recording (for instance the truth of words spoken by the parties whose conversation has been recorded). Where an electronic recorder is used to create information and such evidence is sought to be tendered as truth of content, then the recorded evidence is hearsay (an out-of-court statement tendered as to truth of its content in court) and *prima facie* inadmissible since it cannot be tested by cross-examination of a testifying witness. Thus an interview between police officers and an accused becomes hearsay when the tape is produced as evidence of the truth of the statements recorded. It is original evidence of the fact that the statements were made (see *Maqsud Ali*, page 15). Similarly, a videotaped interview between a social worker, police officer and suspected victim of child abuse is documentary evidence when tendered to prove the truth of the child's assertions. It is perfectly possible, however, that even if it is tendered as hearsay evidence, it will be admissible.

In civil proceedings the tape recordings or video recordings may be relevant in custody, wardship or access disputes, or even in actions by parents against social workers or medical practitioners (the recent Cleveland furore has brought this possibility to the fore). A recording of an incident of public disorder may be relevant in a civil action for assault or other torts against the person. For instance, a journalist may record an incident which will then form the basis of an assault action against the police. In criminal proceedings, the recordings will most commonly be relevant to prove offences through admissions made to the police, but recordings may be used in lieu of the testamentary evidence of witnesses in some circumstances.

In civil proceedings, the Civil Evidence Act 1968 to a large extent abrogates the rule against hearsay evidence. In criminal proceedings the Criminal Justice Act 1988 allows for the reception of hearsay evidence in documentary form in a variety of situations. These two areas are examined in this chapter.

3. Civil proceedings

The Civil Evidence Act 1968 allows for the admission of first hand hearsay, and for the admission of documentary evidence. Section 2 provides that a statement made, whether orally or in a document or otherwise, by any person, whether called as a witness in the proceedings or not, is admissible as evidence of any fact stated therein of which direct oral evidence by that person would be admissible. Section 10 defines "statement" as including any representation of fact whether "made in words or otherwise". "Document" is also defined in s 10 to include the following:

"(a) any map, plan, graph or drawing;

(b) any photograph;

(c) any disc, tape, sound track or other device in which sounds or other data (not being visual images) are embodied so as to be capable (with or without the aid of some other equipment) of being reproduced therefrom; and

(d) any film, negative, tape or other device in which one or more visual images are embodied so as to be capable (as aforesaid) of being reproduced therefrom."

Thus both tape and video recordings are within the definition of "document" under the Act. "Statement" would include not only recorded conversations, but also non-verbal representations of fact such as a video recording showing the gestures of a child during an interview where the child's actions were adduced to demonstrate that sexual abuse had occurred.

(a) First hand hearsay

Although s 2 Civil Evidence Act provides for the general admissibility of first hand hearsay statements, s 8 of the Act and Order 38 Rules of the Supreme Court (or Order 20 of the County Court Rules in county court proceedings) lay down the specific conditions that must be followed before such hearsay evidence can be admitted. Further, where it is intended to call the maker of the statement as a witness in addition to admitting the statement itself in evidence, leave of the court is necessary before the statement can be adduced (s 2(2)(a)).

Admissibility under the Act depends upon the service of notices and (where appropriate) counter-notices by the parties. It is convenient to outline the procedure in numbered stages as follows:

(i) Order 38 rule 21 requires the service of a notice by the party wishing to adduce hearsay evidence, within twenty-one days of (a) setting down for trial or hearing or adjournment into court; or (b) appointment for the first hearing; or (c) within such period as the court may specify. This procedure does not apply to affidavits (O 38 r 21(4)), but does apply to any document exhibited with an affidavit.

(ii) By Order 38 rule 22(2), if the statement is admissible by virtue of s 2 and was made in a document, a copy or transcript of the document, or the relevant part thereof must be annexed to the notice. If certain matters are not apparent on the face of the document, then they must be stated in the notice. These matters are the time, place and circumstances in which the statement was made, and the person(s) by whom and to whom it was made.

(iii) If it is not intended to call the witness to give evidence, the notice must also specify the reasons why the witness cannot or should not be called. The reasons are set out in O 38 r 25 and s 8(2)(b) of the Act and are that the witness:

- is dead; or
- is beyond the seas; or

- is unfit by reason of bodily or mental condition to attend as a witness; or
- cannot with reasonable diligence be identified or found or cannot reasonably be expected (having regard to the time which has elapsed and to all the circumstances) to have any recollection of matters relevant to the accuracy or otherwise of the statement.

Similar reasons apply in criminal proceedings; (see page 25).

(iv) A counter-notice must be served if the other side requires the witness to be called. If no reason under r 25 (above) applies, then failure to comply with the counter-notice results in the inadmissibility of the statement (r 25(4)). This is subject to the overriding discretion of the court to admit the statement notwithstanding that there has been a failure to comply with the requirements of notice or counter-notice (r 29 and s 8(3)(a) of the Act). If a reason under r 25 applies, then a counter-notice can be served only if the party requiring the attendance of the witness contends that the witness can or should be called (r 26(2)).

(b) The weight to be attached to the statement

Section 6 of the Civil Evidence Act provides that in estimating the weight, if any, to be attached to a statement admissible by virtue of s 2, regard shall be had to "all the circumstances from which an inference can reasonably be drawn as to the accuracy or otherwise of the statement". In particular the court will have regard to whether or not the statement was made contemporaneously with the occurrence or existence of the facts stated, and to whether the maker of the statement had any incentive to conceal or misrepresent the facts. Therefore, as with recordings adduced as original evidence, weight and admissibility are separate issues. The quality of electronically recorded evidence will obviously be a matter affecting weight, since it may well affect the accuracy of the statement relied upon.

Section 7 of the Act provides for the admission of evidence to destroy or support the credibility of the maker of a statement who is not called as a witness. Thus the credibility of a witness can be challenged even though he is not called to give evidence. Section 7 also allows for proof of the inconsistency of statements made by the person whose statement is tendered in evidence. The purpose of proving such inconsistency is to show that that person has "contradicted himself". Thus although hearsay evidence may be admitted, it does not follow that it will carry any more weight than if the maker had himself been called to give evidence and had been subjected to cross-examination by the other side.

(c) Admissions

Section 9 of the Civil Evidence Act preserves pre-existing common law exceptions to the hearsay rule. No notice is required in respect of such evidence. The admissibility conditions of s 2 of the Act do not apply. The exception relevant to electronically recorded evidence is that of an admission adverse to a party to the proceedings, whether made by that party or by another person (s 9(2)(a)). Such an admission may be given in evidence "for the purpose of proving any fact stated in the admission". Thus an admission of liability made by a potential defendant in an interview conducted and recorded by a journalist would be admissible without notice in any subsequent action against him, for instance in a personal injury action based on an alleged breach of duty of care of an employer, or negligence of a manufacturer. Similarly an admission made by a parent as to abuse of a child recorded during an interview with a social worker would be admissible in subsequent wardship proceedings.

The admission might also be made by someone "in privity" with the defendant. Such admissions are sometimes called vicarious admissions. Someone "in privity" includes, for example, an agent of the defendant and an employee. Thus an employee might give a recorded interview to a journalist, the content of which forms an admission against his employer; a salesman might, for instance, make a statement concerning goods or services which is admissible as evidence against his employer in an action based on breach of contract or misrepresentation. However, it is important to note that the statement itself must be made in the course of duty; that is, the making of the admission must be within the scope of the agent's authority. If such an admission is made outside the scope of the agent's authority the statement may none the less be admissible under s 2 Civil Evidence Act. The notice procedure must therefore be used and the employer might well serve a counter-notice requiring the witness to be called. Such a witness might prove hostile to the party calling him. Order 38 r 29(2) provides that the court may admit a statement under s 2 (notwithstanding any failure to comply with the notice procedures) if refusal to admit it might oblige the party desiring to give the statement in evidence to call as a witness "an opposite party or a person who was at the material time the servant or agent of an opposite party".

(d) Records as evidence of facts stated

Section 4 of the Civil Evidence Act allows for the admission of statements contained in documents in certain cases. Where s 4 applies, multiple hearsay may be admitted. A multiple hearsay statement is an out-of-court statement that has been repeated to more than one person sequentially before it is finally adduced in evidence. The requirements of s 4 are that:

(i) the statement is contained in a document;
(ii) the document is or forms part of a record;
(iii) the record is compiled by a person acting under a duty;
(iv) the information was supplied by a person (whether acting under a duty or not) who had or may reasonably be supposed to have had personal knowledge of the matters dealt with in that information;
(v) if the information was not supplied directly to the compiler of the record, but was supplied indirectly through intermediaries, each intermediary must be acting under a duty to record.

Section 4(3) defines "duty" to include "any trade, business, profession or other occupation". It includes any paid or unpaid office. The same notice requirements, and provisions as to assessing the weight to be attached to the statement, apply as in the case of first hand hearsay statements under s 2 of the Act (see pages 20 to 22). In many instances in civil proceedings, there will be an overlap between s 2 and 4 of the Act.

Thus an interview between a social worker and child or parent, which has been recorded on video tape, may be admitted under either section, so long as the provisions of s 8 and O 38 are complied with. The recording is a document within s 10. The record is compiled under a duty (the social worker's professional duty), from information supplied by someone with personal knowledge (the child, the parent, or perhaps the social worker).

The term "record" is not defined in the Act. In *H* v *Schering Chemicals* (1983) it was stated that a "record" within s 4 of the Act was either a document that gave effect to a transaction, or a contemporaneous register of information supplied by those with direct knowledge of the facts. Thus in the instant case summaries of the results of research, and articles and letters published in medical journals, concerning a drug which was alleged to have caused personal injury, were not records within the section. The decision follows the case of *Re Koscot Interplanetary (UK) Ltd* (1972) where Mr Justice Megarry doubted whether a summary of proceedings that had been taken or were contemplated in United States courts against an American company could amount to a "record".

He further emphasised that the document must have been prepared by an identified person (it would be impossible to say otherwise whether that person was acting under a duty in recording the information). It was said that if the identity of the compiler of the record were unknown "it may well be that questions arise not merely on hearsay, but also (if I may say so) on whosay". (per Megarry J)

In the case of electronically recorded evidence, the identity of the supplier of the information will be obvious in most cases. The identity of the creator of the recording must also, however, always be ascertained to comply with s 4. Because of the overlap between ss 2 and 4 of the Act, less use may be made of s 4 in the context of video or tape recorded evidence. Its significance in relation to such evidence is that it has formed the model for recent statutory evidence exceptions to the hearsay rule in criminal cases. Those exceptions were first enacted in s 68 Police and Criminal Evidence Act 1984. They have been further extended by the Criminal Justice Act 1988 (repealing s 68 PACE). The Criminal Justice Act is now considered.

4. Criminal proceedings

The Criminal Justice Act 1988 provides for the reception of first hand hearsay, and for the reception of "business documents" when certain criteria are satisfied; these criteria are very similar to those under the Civil Evidence Act.

(a) First hand hearsay

Section 23 of the Act, in force from 2 April 1989, provides for the admissibility in criminal proceedings of a statement made by a person in a "document". By virtue of Sch 2 para 5, the definition of document is identical with that contained in s 10 of the Civil Evidence Act (see page 19). Tapes and video tapes are therefore documents within s 23. The statement will be admissible in criminal proceedings as "evidence of any fact of which direct oral evidence . . . would be admissible", if one of the requirements of s 23(2) or (3) is complied with.

Section 23(2) lists the following criteria (they are disjunctive, that is, only one need be satisfied):

- (i) that the person who made the statement is dead or by reason of his bodily or mental condition unfit to attend as a witness; *or*
- (ii) that the person who made the statement is outside the UK and it is not reasonably practicable to secure his attendance; *or*
- (iii) that all reasonable steps have been taken to find the person who made the statement, but that he cannot be found.

There are three differences between these grounds for admission of hearsay evidence and those applicable in civil proceedings. Firstly, under the exception relating to witnesses outside the UK, the witness must not only be beyond the seas: it must also be impracticable to secure his attendance. In *R* v *Bray* (1988) it was stated that the issue of whether it was reasonable to secure the attendance of a witness was not to be examined at the moment that the trial opened, but was to be examined against the whole background of the case. Thus a witness who had been out of the jurisdiction for seven months prior to the trial should have been contacted in advance of the hearing to secure his attendance. It is less likely that electronic recordings of the statements of key witnesses will be admitted under this section, since video links may well be used in such cases (see s 32 Criminal Justice Act, page 7 *et seq*). However, since the use of video links is entirely at the discretion of the court and since not every Crown Court will be so equipped, it is conceivable that recordings could be tendered in evidence on this ground. There is provision in s 29 of the Act for evidence to be taken by a court or appropriate authority outside the jurisdiction at the request of prosecution or defence. There seems to be no reason why this evidence could not be electronically recorded. Indeed it would create a far more accurate picture of the testimony, especially where the statement was challenged by questioning the person who made it.

The second difference is that in a criminal case the identity of the maker of the statement must be known. In other words, it is not a ground for admission that he cannot be identified, only that he cannot be found. This is of little importance in the context of electronically recorded evidence.

The third difference is that in criminal cases it is *not* a ground of admissibility that the maker of the statement cannot be expected (having regard to the time which has elapsed and to all the circumstances) to have any recollection of matters relevant to the accuracy or otherwise of the statement. This is a substantial difference, because in practice it forms the basis for the admission of a large part of hearsay evidence. It is, however, a ground for admission in the case of business documents (see page 29).

Section 23(3) sets out the other basis for the admission of first hand hearsay; it provides for the admissibility of a statement made to a police officer or some other person charged with the duty of investigating offences or charging offences (for example, Customs and Excise officers), where the person who made the statement does not appear to give oral evidence through fear or because he is kept out of the way. Thus if the police interview suspects and tape record such interviews, the statement of a suspect who has been dealt with, or who is not proceeded against (and, in either case, is therefore competent for the prosecution), would be admissible under this section if fear could be proved. This might well be relevant where the suspect is "turning Queen's evidence" against an associate. In this way an out-of-court statement against a co-accused could become admissible once the accused had been separately dealt with (for example, by pleading guilty or by being acquitted). The statement would be original evidence as to the fact that the interview took place and that the words were spoken. It would be documentary if it was sought to rely on the truth of what was said. It should be noted that s 76 PACE (requiring the prosecution to show that a confession was not made under oppression or in such circumstances that it is unreliable) applies notwithstanding s 23 Criminal Justice Act. Thus a confession obtained in breach of the Codes of Practice under PACE might well be excluded under s 76, even though it would otherwise be admissible under s 23 Criminal Justice Act. Discretion to exclude first hand hearsay on the basis of the interests of justice is dealt with later in this chapter; see page 30 *et seq*.

(b) Business documents

Section 24 of the Criminal Justice Act provides that a statement in a document is admissible in criminal proceedings as evidence of any fact of which direct oral evidence would be admissible if:

(i) the document was created or received by a person in the course of a trade, business or profession or other occupation or as the holder of a paid or unpaid office; *and*

(ii) the information contained in the document was supplied by a person (whether or not the maker of

> the statement) who had or may reasonably be supposed to have had personal knowledge of the matters dealt with. If the information was supplied indirectly, each person through whom it was supplied must have received it in the course of a trade, business profession or other occupation or as the holder of a paid or unpaid office.

The following matters should be noted in respect of s 24. Firstly, there is a provision identical with that contained in s 23, preserving the requirements of s 76 PACE (see above, and also Chapter 6). Secondly, subject to a discretion to exclude the statement in the interests of justice (see page 30 *et seq*), there are no further conditions for the admissibility of business documents unless they are prepared for the purposes of pending or contemplated criminal proceedings or for the purposes of criminal investigation. Thus a video recording of an interview with a customer made by a journalist for the purpose of a television broadcast highlighting unscrupulous retail trade practices would in all probability be admissible in any subsequent criminal proceedings brought against the retailer for breach of the Trades Descriptions Act 1972 or under the Consumer Protection Act 1987. No conditions as to the non-availability of the witness need be satisfied. Similarly, an interview between a social worker or a child psychologist and a child, undertaken merely to establish why patterns of problem behaviour were emerging, would probably be admissible in any subsequent proceedings for abuse which resulted from disclosures made in the interview. In both these examples, the creator of the recording would be acting in the course of a profession or other occupation and the information would have been supplied by a person who might reasonably be supposed to have personal knowledge of the matters dealt with in the statement.

There is no statutory definition of the circumstances in which a document is "prepared for the purposes of" criminal proceedings or a criminal investigation. No doubt case law will evolve to define these issues more precisely. However, it is suggested that a test similar to that applied in ascertaining the existence of legal professional privilege will be relevant. The courts will look to see what is the dominant purpose of the recording, rather than whether the recording was brought into existence solely for the purpose of criminal litigation. This would accord with the majority view in *Waugh* v *BRB* (1979), which was a case concerning legal professional privilege (that is, privilege from disclosing the documentation in question to the other side in the proceedings). It is to be noted that Lord Denning gave a dissenting judgment in this case and considered that to claim privilege the document must have been brought into existence wholly or mainly for the purpose of litigation or legal advice. The matter is not, therefore, totally free from doubt. In any event, it may be a moot point in a situation such as an interview between social worker and child at what stage the interview becomes one prepared for the purposes of a criminal investigation or proceedings.

If a document is prepared for the purpose of proceedings or investigation, then one of the conditions in s 23(2) or (3) (discussed above) must be satisfied before the evidence can be admitted. Alternatively, s 24(4)(iii) must be satisfied. This is the condition (absent from first hand hearsay statements) that the person who made the statement cannot reasonably be expected (having regard to the time which has elapsed since he made the statement and to all the circumstances) to have any recollection of the matters dealt with in the statement.

The particular usefulness of s 24(4)(iii) in the context of electronically recorded evidence, might well be to provide evidence of an out-of-court identification (made at an identification parade or group identification) in a case where the witness cannot recollect that he identified the accused previously, and fails to make an in-court (dock) identification. A group identification differs from a parade in that the suspect is placed among a crowd of people (for instance, on a railway platform or in a shopping precinct). It may take place because an identity parade is impracticable. This might occur where, because of the ethnic origin of the suspect or because of some physical peculiarity, it is not possible to bring together for a parade eight people of similar age, height, general appearance and position in life to the suspect, as required by the Codes of Practice made pursuant to PACE.

Proof of such an out-of-court identification has, in the past, been admitted through the oral testimony of a police officer to the effect that the witness did in fact identify the accused prior to the trial: *R* v *Osbourne and Virtue* (1973). However, such testimony has always been regarded as evidentially suspect in that it amounts to hearsay evidence. The officer is giving evidence of an assertion made by the identifying witness to the effect that that witness picked out the accused as the man he had sighted committing the crime. This assertion was made out of court (at the parade or group identification), and yet the officer is testifying to its truthfulness. If a video recording of the parade were to be admitted under s 24 of the Criminal Justice Act, it would no longer be evidentially suspect. It would fall within a recognised exception to the hearsay rule in that it was a document created in the course of an occupation (that of police officer), from information supplied by a person who had personal knowledge of the matters dealt with (the witness). The recording would have the further advantage of being available as evidence which the court could view and assess. The degree of certainty or otherwise with which the witness identified the suspect would be apparent.

The law relating to the admission of documentary evidence in criminal proceedings has been simplified by the Criminal Justice Act to the extent that the document no longer has to constitute a "record" to be admissible. Thus a police witness statement which is recorded on tape or video tape should be admissible (contrast *R* v *O'Laughlin* (1987)), providing that the other requirements of the Act, as discussed in this chapter, are complied with. An identification made by a witness is no different from any other witness statement. It should therefore, in almost all cases, be possible to adduce evidence of what occurred at an identification parade where that parade has been recorded, either to show the process of identification (see page 5); or to show that an identification was in fact made, in a case where the witness fails to remember whom he identified at the parade or group identification.

(c) The interests of justice criterion

The Criminal Justice Act provides for safeguards to prevent

the reception of hearsay evidence where it would not be in the interests of justice to do so. Both ss 23 and 24 are subject to these provisions. Section 25 provides that the court has an inherent discretion not to admit a statement otherwise admissible under the above sections if it "is of the opinion that in the interests of justice" it should not be so admitted. In assessing the interests of justice the court must have regard, *inter alia*, to:

(i) the nature and source of the document and whether or not it is likely that the document is authentic;
(ii) the extent to which the statement appears to supply evidence which would not otherwise be readily available;
(iii) the relevance of the evidence to any issue in the proceedings;
(iv) the risk of unfairness to the accused, particularly where it is not possible to controvert the statement if the person making it does not attend to give evidence in the proceedings.

This last factor is likely to be of the greatest significance where the court is relying substantially on the hearsay testimony of a prosecution witness.

Section 26 provides for a virtually identical safeguard whenever documents (other than expert reports and letters of request to a foreign court or authority to obtain evidence) are prepared for the purpose of criminal proceedings or a criminal investigation. Such evidence shall only be admissible with leave of the court. Leave will only be given if the court is of the opinion that it ought to be admitted in the interests of justice. The court will have regard to:

(i) the contents of the statement;
(ii) any risk of unfairness to the accused (particularly where it is not possible to controvert the statement); and
(iii) any other circumstances that appear to the court to be relevant.

There is clearly a substantial overlap between ss 25 and 26 of the Act. It is suggested that essentially the distinction affects the burden on the party seeking to admit the statement. If the document has been made for the purpose of criminal proceedings or a criminal investigation, then the party wishing to adduce it in evidence must convince the court that it is in the interests of justice to do so. Otherwise it will not be admitted, since leave of the court is necessary. If the document has not been so made, leave is not necessary and the party objecting to its admission in evidence on the basis that it is against the interests of justice to do so, will have to raise this question before the court.

It should be noted that under Sch 2 of the Act, where hearsay evidence is admitted, the credibility of the maker of the statement may be impugned. This may be done by adducing evidence, with leave of the court, of any matter upon which (if that person had been called as a witness) he could have been cross-examined concerning his credibility or by providing a previous inconsistent statement. In attaching weight to the statement, account will be taken of all the circumstances, including inferences to be drawn from its accuracy or otherwise.

Since there is a general discretion to prevent the admission of documents containing hearsay statements as above, it may be that applications by the defence for the court to exclude evidence under s 78 PACE (see page 14 *et seq*) will be based upon the same arguments and to that extent will be unlikely to succeed where the interests of justice test is satisfied.

Applications to exclude could still be made on the basis of s 78, since s 28 Criminal Justice Act preserves the existing discretion of the court to exclude any evidence which would otherwise be admissible as hearsay evidence. The most common ground for seeking exclusion under s 78 PACE arises where there has been a breach of the rules concerning the detention and interrogation of suspects, and this is considered in more detail in Chapter 6 (dealing with the tape recording of police interviews).

(d) Proof of documents

The "best evidence" rule (see page 9) has no application under the Criminal Justice Act. Section 27 provides that where a statement in a document is admissible under the

Act, it may be proved either by production of that document or (whether or not that document is still in existence) by the production of a copy of that document or the material part of it. The document or the copy must be authenticated in such manner as the court may approve. It is "immaterial" how many removes there are between the copy and the original. Nonetheless, a poor quality copy tape will carry little weight and might even be excluded under the interests of justice test above. As stated in Chapter 1, specific rules apply to copy tapes taken of police interviews.

Chapter 3

Child witnesses

1. Recording interviews on video tape

Video recordings are increasingly used by both social workers and child psychologists as a means of documenting interviews which take place with children suspected of having been abused. Most of the reported cases have involved allegations of sexual abuse rather than physical abuse *simpliciter*. This is due to the pioneering use of video recordings together with sexually explicit dolls in the investigation of sexual abuse. These interview aids, used initially by Great Ormond Street Children's Hospital, are now widely used throughout the country. It should be emphasised, however, that although the cases referred to throughout this chapter relate to sexual abuse, the potential of video recorded evidence has a far wider application. It allows a child witness statement to be given in relatively relaxed and spontaneous circumstances. There are, however, privacy implications in that the child is, at present, not always aware that the recording is taking place. This matter is dealt with in Chapter 5, which discusses in full the privacy issues of electronically recorded evidence. Further, the purpose of the interview itself may well be other than to provide evidence in court proceedings; for example, it may be to investigate parental concerns over a child. The style of questioning may therefore be inappropriate for the courtroom; for instance, it may contain leading questions, that is, questions which suggest an answer, and are not acceptable in court.

The problem of interviewing children for diagnostic purposes is dealt with later in this chapter. In civil proceedings, the video recorded evidence of children may be adduced in wardship hearings or in custody or access disputes. In criminal proceedings such evidence may be relevant in deciding whether to prefer charges relating to sexual offences against a parent or other person. To date, such evidence has not been adduced in a criminal trial.

2. Wardship and custody proceedings

In both wardship and custody hearings in the High Court and county court, evidence is in the first instance given by way of affidavits filed in court. Documents upon which a party intends to rely should be exhibited with the affidavit evidence. The court will require oral evidence from the person seeking care and control of the child. Indeed the Matrimonial Causes Rules provide that in deciding custody and access on divorce, the judge may refuse to admit the affidavit of any person with whom the child is living or with whom it is proposed the child should live, or who is, or is proposed to be, responsible for the child's welfare, unless that person is available to give oral evidence. In the magistrates' court, only oral evidence can be received. In all courts the relevant rules of evidence have *prima facie* application to hearings concerning the custody and welfare of children. The admission of hearsay evidence in the High Court and county court is thus, in principle, governed by the Civil Evidence Act 1968 (see Chapter 2). The Civil Evidence Act does not apply in the magistrates' court, however. The principle that the child's welfare is paramount requires the court to have regard to all the evidence available, even if the only evidence is hearsay, provided that proper notice is given so that it can be challenged.

In the case of *Re K (Infants)* (1965), the House of Lords stated that an inflexible rule against hearsay is quite unsuited to the exercise of a parental and administrative jurisdiction. The judge in chambers could assess what weight should be attached to hearsay evidence. Thus, even before the Civil Evidence Act 1968, hearsay evidence in questions of wardship or custody was a matter of weight rather than of admissibility. This principle was restated in the case of *In Re N (Minors) (Wardship: Evidence)* (1987). It was stated that it was well settled in children's cases that the court should not exclude hearsay evidence, but should carefully assess the weight to be attached to such indirect evidence. Where an allegation was made against a parent, the original source of information should depose in his affidavit that he was prepared to attend for cross-examination. Thus a distinction may be made between matters of hearsay evidence which are not likely to be challenged and those which are a component part of allegations against a parent or other person. Video taped evidence is almost certain to be within the latter category, in that it will contain allegations concerning an individual. In the apparently aberrant case of *Re D (A Minor) (Wardship: Evidence)* (1986) hearsay evidence (notes taken by a solicitor, in connection with divorce proceedings, of a conversation with the child's mother) was held to be inadmissible. However, the notes contained serious allegations against the father and his family and therefore it is in line with authority that they should have been excluded. It was held in *Re D* that neither s 2 nor s 4 of the Civil Evidence Act applied on the facts of the case. The child's mother had died and the notes taken by the solicitor were the only evidence of her assertions against the father.

However, even if the video recorded evidence contains allegations against a person involved in the proceedings, it may be admitted in the following ways:

(a) pursuant to s 2 or 4 Civil Evidence Act 1968; or
(b) by agreement; or
(c) as original rather than hearsay documentary evidence.

These three possibilities are examined below.

(a) Sections 2 and 4 Civil Evidence Act 1968

As stated in Chapter 2 (see page 19), video tapes are documents within the Civil Evidence Act. Section 2 will permit the statement to be admitted in evidence by agreement under the notice procedure. Alternatively, one of the grounds specified in s 8 and Order 38 Rules of the Supreme Court may apply. If the child is the relevant witness, the most likely possible ground of admission is that he is unfit by reason of bodily or mental condition to attend as a witness. Surprisingly, it does not seem that there is any judicial interpretation of the applicability of this ground in relation to a child witness who might *suffer trauma* by giving evidence, but does not suffer from mental or physical illness. There seems no reason in principle, however, why on the literal reading of this provision, this should not be a frequently used basis for the admission of video recorded evidence both under the Civil Evidence Act and under the Criminal Justice Act 1988 (see page 39). Section 4 is subject to the same restraints of admissibility as s 2. As stated in Chapter 2, the sections will (in the context of electronically recorded evidence) usually be interchangeable.

(b) By agreement

In all the wardship cases which are cited in this chapter concerning the problem of techniques to be adopted when interviewing a child witness, the video recording was admitted by the agreement of the parties. The principle of paramountcy of the child's welfare has thus led to the admission of this evidence, even when one party is thereby accused of improper or illegal sexual behaviour. However, the fact that the tape is admitted does not prevent the accused party from challenging the interpretation of the child's evidence made by a psychologist or psychiatrist and thereby challenging the fact that abuse took place (see page 50).

(c) As original evidence

So far it has been assumed that the video recorded evidence of an interview will be hearsay evidence. The child is not called to court to testify, and usually the truth of the assertions made by the child is the issue in the case. However, in the case of *Bolton Metropolitan Borough Council* v *W* (1988), video recordings of access visits between a mother and her children, who were wards of court and in local authority care, were held to be original evidence. The case in fact turned on the question of privilege—whether the local authority was bound to show the tapes to the mother's legal advisors. It was held that the tapes should be disclosed and that they were not within the same category as social work reports. They were simply "audible and visible records of events in which the persons in dispute played no part in producing". The video recorder was simply used as a recording device and did not create information, the truth of which could be disputed. An interview between social worker and child, or between psychologist and child, does create information rather than simply record a spontaneous interchange. If the assertions of the child, rather than their truth, are relied upon, the evidence will not be hearsay since it will be tendered simply to show that the statements were made. It is unlikely that assertions made in response to direct questioning will be of much evidential weight, however, unless their truth is also established.

3. Criminal proceedings

(a) Evidence before trial

In order to decide whether criminal charges should be preferred, the police may wish to view evidence which has been obtained by interviews, conducted by others, of victims of suspected abuse. Whether they can do so, once the children have been made wards of court, depends upon the decision of the court. It does not depend upon the decision of the party (such as a local authority) to whose care the ward is committed: *Re S (Minors) (Wardship: Police Investigation)* (1987). In that case it was said that the court will weigh the public need to give protection against offenders, against the need of the individual ward and the consequential involvement of the ward in criminal proceedings. The question of whether the police can seize video tapes of such interviews against the wishes of social workers or psychologists is discussed in Chapter 4, which deals with privilege and disclosure issues relating to electronically recorded evidence generally.

(b) Evidence in the course of proceedings

Video recorded evidence of child victim interviews is currently regarded as inadmissible in criminal trials on the basis that it is hearsay; and that in charges as grave as those involving sexual offences with children, the orality of trial should be preserved and the accused should not be denied the right to cross-examine his accuser. Lord Hailsham stated, in debate on the Criminal Justice Act 1988, that the admission of such evidence would undermine both the burden and standard of proof for a conviction for a detestable crime. At various stages of the parliamentary debates preceding the Act, amendments were proposed to provide for the admission of such evidence. Sir Eldon Griffiths unsuccessfully sought to move an amendment which would have allowed in evidence a video recording of an interview with a child under fourteen years, provided that the recorded evidence could then be tested in court by cross-examination. Such cross-examination would have been relayed to the child through a "prescribed officer of the court" by means of a video link. As was pointed out in debate, the child would not be saved the trauma of cross-examination and, indeed, might be put under even greater pressure in having to avoid inconsistencies between the recorded statement and answers given in cross-examination. The debate on this amendment took place in the wake of the Cleveland controversy. Mr Stuart Bell (campaigner on behalf of parents in Cleveland who alleged that their children had been wrongly diagnosed as being sexually abused) pointed out the questionable quality of interviewing skills possessed by social workers and the extreme pressure felt by some children to disclose abuse or face permanent separation from their parents. In the extremely sensitive climate then prevailing, it is hardly surprising that the amendment was withdrawn.

It is possible, however, that such evidence might be admissible as documentary hearsay under s 23 or 24 Criminal Justice Act 1988. As stated earlier in this chapter, it is arguable that, if the child will suffer psychological disturbance or trauma by giving evidence, he is unfit by reason of bodily or mental condition to attend as a witness. This would satisfy an admission requirement under s 23 of the Act (first hand hearsay; see page 25 *et seq*); or s 24 of the Act (business documents; see page 27 *et seq*) where the document is prepared for the purpose of a criminal investigation or proceedings. The video recording could be either a first hand hearsay statement; or a business document—the information has been supplied by someone with personal knowledge and is recorded by someone in the course of a profession or other occupation. If it is established that the video recording was not made for the purpose of a criminal investigation or proceedings, it will be admissible as a business document without the need to satisfy a specific admission requirement. At what stage an interview is deemed to be made for the purpose of a criminal investigation is a matter yet to be decided. It may well depend not so much on the strict chronology of events as upon the nature of the interview, that is, whether it is a formal interview to hear what the child has to say or a "facilitative" interview held for therapeutic purposes (see interviewing techniques, page 45 *et seq*). However, the interests of justice criteria in ss 25 and 26 of the Act (see page 30 *et seq*) will apply in these situations. A man who stands accused of a serious crime on the basis of a recorded interview may well argue that there is a risk of unfairness in that he will be unable to controvert the statement. The interviewing techniques adopted would also be relevant to the issue of whether it was in the interests of justice to admit the statement as hearsay evidence.

(c) Closed circuit television links

Section 32 of the Criminal Justice Act provides for the reception of evidence from a child under fourteen years by closed circuit television link, when the child is a witness to a charge involving a sexual offence or an offence of violence or cruelty in relation to children (see page 7 *et seq*). The child is thus spared the trauma of facing his or her alleged abuser in court, but is still available for cross-examination during the course of the trial. The television link is "live" and the child's response to cross-examination and his demeanour are visible to all those present in the court room. Thus the evidence will only become electronically recorded if, after the completion of the trial, a video recording of the child's testimony is provided, in addition to the transcript, on appeal. The use of closed circuit television links commenced in January 1989.

The Crown Court (Amendment) (No 5) Rules 1988 (SI 1988 No 2160) lay down rules of court governing the giving of evidence through television link where the witness is under fourteen. The Crown Court Rules 1982 have been amended thereby by the insertion of a new Rule 23A. Rule 23A(1) provides that any party may apply for leave under s 32(1) of the Act for evidence to be so given. Rule 23A(2) states that such application shall be made by giving notice in writing which shall be in the form prescribed in Sch 5 "or a form to like effect". The prescribed form is reproduced on page 43. By Rule 23A(3), the application must be made within twenty-eight days after the date of the committal of the defendant or, as the case may be, of consent to the preferral of a bill of indictment in relation to the case. The notice must be sent to the appropriate officer of the Crown Court and a copy is sent by the applicant to "every other party to the proceedings" (Rule 23A(4)). The period of twenty-eight days may be extended (either before or after it expires) by an application in writing to the Crown Court and notice to every other party. An application for extension of time is determined by a Crown Court judge.

If a party who has received a copy of a notice for leave to give evidence under s 32(1) wishes to oppose the application, he must, within fourteen days, notify the applicant and the appropriate officer of the court in writing of his opposition and give reasons therefor (Rule 23A(5)). Whether or not an application is to be determined by a hearing is entirely a matter for the discretion of the judge. If the judge does direct that a hearing is to take place, the appropriate officer of the Crown Court shall notify the parties of the time and place of the hearing (Rule 23A(6)). In any event, Rule 23A(7) states that the parties shall be notified by the Crown Court officer of a decision made in relation to an application under s 32(1) Criminal Justice Act. Further, where leave is granted, the notification shall state:

"(a) where the witness is to give evidence on behalf of the prosecutor, the name of the witness, and if known, the name, occupation and relationship (if any) to the witness of the person who is to accompany the witness and,

(b) the location of the Crown Court at which the trial should take place".

The rules appear to leave all matters relating to the reception of evidence through live television link in these circumstances to the discretion of the judge. Rule 23A(10) provides that:

> "a witness under the age of 14 shall, when giving evidence through a television link, be accompanied by a person acceptable to a judge of the Crown Court and, unless the judge otherwise directs, by no other person".

The question of who is to accompany the child witness is a crucial aspect of the procedure. The defence may well not object to evidence being given by television link, but may object to a particular person accompanying the child whilst this is done. It may be alleged that the person is capable of influencing the child by gesture or expression or simply by his or her presence in the room. This argument might be raised against a parent of the child or a social worker who has previously conducted interviews with the child in relation to the alleged sexual offences. Schedule 5 requires the applicant to state the name of the person who is proposed to accompany the witness, the occupation of this person and his or her relationship to the witness. The judge is clearly entitled to veto this proposal, since he has absolute discretion under Rule 23(A)(10) as to who should accompany the child. A potential difficulty exists to the extent that the child is likely to feel most comfortable and relaxed with a parent or social worker previously known to him or her. However, it is exactly these persons who are most likely (even unwittingly) to influence the child in giving evidence. It has certainly been stated (see *C* v *C (Child Abuse: Evidence)* (1987), page 49 below) that a parent should not be present during an interview held by a psychologist for the purpose of establishing whether sexual abuse has occurred. If the danger of the parent influencing the child is present when a video recorded interview takes place, then it is equally present and rather more crucial when the child is giving evidence in criminal proceedings.

When a child gives evidence by closed circuit television, such testimony will no longer need to be corroborated, if unsworn. Section 34(1) Criminal Justice Act 1988 provides:

> "The proviso to subsection (1) of section 38 of the

Notice of Application for leave to use television link where witness is under the age of 14, under Section 32(1)(b) of the Criminal Justice Act 1988

- An application should be made within **28 days** after the day on which the case was committed for trial **or** of consent to the preferral of a bill of indictment in relation to the case. This form may also be used where an extension of time has been granted for the making of this application.
- A copy of this form must be given at the same time to the other party or parties to the case.

* delete as appropriate

Case Details

The Crown Court at   Crown Court Case Number:

Date of: committal for trial*:
consent to preferral of bill of indictment*:

State the name(s) of the defendant(s) **to whom this application relates**

Defendant(s) Surname: Forenames:

Application

Name of Applicant:

Name of Applicant's Solicitor:

Address of Solicitor:

Reference:

Give brief details of those charges **to which this application applies**

Charges

Note:
An application by the defence for evidence to be given through live television link need not disclose who that witness is **except** to the extent that disclosure is required by Section 11 of the Criminal Justice Act 1967 (alibi) **nor** need it disclose the name of the person proposed to accompany the witness if this could lead to the identification of the witness.

Witness • Please read the **Note** beside this section before completing it.

Date of Birth:

If the Applicant is the prosecutor enter the name of the witness (otherwise leave blank):

Name of the person who is **proposed** to accompany the witness:

Occupation of **this** person:

Relation to the witness of **this** person:

Grounds for applying

Signature of applicant
or
applicant's solicitor   Date

....

> Children and Young Persons Act 1933 (under which, where the unsworn evidence of a child of tender years admitted by virtue of that section is given on behalf of the prosecution, the accused is not liable to be convicted unless that evidence is corroborated by some other material evidence in support thereof implicating him) shall cease to have effect."

Thus a child will only have to appreciate the duty to tell the truth in order to give evidence under s 38 of the Children and Young Persons Act 1933. There is no longer any need to establish that the child can also appreciate the additional obligation of giving evidence on oath. The absence of corroborative evidence will not invalidate the child's testimony.

Section 34(2) of the Criminal Justice Act states that:

> "Any requirement whereby at a trial on indictment it is obligatory for the court to give the jury a warning about convicting the accused on the uncorroborated evidence of a child is abrogated in relation to cases where such a warning is required by reason only that the evidence is the evidence of a child."

Thus a warning as to the dangers of convicting on the evidence of children, where such evidence is sworn but uncorroborated, is no longer necessary. It is to be noted, however, that where the child is a victim of a sexual offence (as will usually be the case when the child gives evidence by closed circuit television link) there is still the need for a warning to the jury that it is not safe to convict on the uncorroborated evidence of the complainant of a sexual offence. The fact that the child repeats the complaint many times is not corroboration. However, if a witness sees a child in a distressed condition immediately after the alleged incident, this might amount to corroboration, if in the circumstances the child is not making a complaint of abuse and has no idea that he or she is being observed (*R* v *Redpath* (1962). In many cases there will be medical evidence to corroborate what the child is saying. It must be remembered, in any event, that in the case of sexual offences it is the *warning* that is mandatory and not the corroborating evidence. Thus a jury may still convict upon the evidence, without corroboration, if satisfied that the testimony is true.

Section 34(3) Criminal Justice Act provides that the unsworn testimony of a child can corroborate either sworn or unsworn evidence given by any person. Two children, who both give unsworn testimony because they are too young to take the oath, can now corroborate one another.

4. Interviewing techniques

The interviewing techniques used by those questioning possible victims of sexual abuse will depend upon the purpose for which the interview is conducted. There are essentially two kinds of interview. The first is referred to in the *Report of the Inquiry into Child Abuse in Cleveland 1987* as a "formal interview". The purpose of such an interview is to listen to the child and thereby to establish what the child wishes to say in an unprompted and voluntary statement. Although those questioning the child must be skilled in interviewing children and sensitive to their needs, the Report concludes that:

> "From all the evidence provided to the Inquiry there is no reason whatsoever to conclude that the police officer, often a policewoman, and the social worker are other than entirely suitable professionals to interview such children, provided they have the appropriate training and interviewing skills." (para. 12.12 of the Report.)

It is not the purpose of a formal interview to give therapy to the child in question. Such interviews should therefore contain no leading or hypothetical questions, promptings or other pressures designed to force the child to disclose abuse. Thus in theory formal interviews can be conducted so that a video recording of such an interview could be tendered in court and have evidential weight attached to it. One of the statutory exceptions to the hearsay rule would, of course, have to apply (see page 25), or the recording could be admitted by agreement.

The second kind of interview is referred to in the Report as "facilitative". The Report states that this interview takes place as a second stage in the proceedings, "where the assessment to that date is inconclusive". It is recognised that in conducting this interview, use may be made of hypothetical or leading questions. It is stressed in the Report that the facilitative stage should not be seen as a routine part of the general interview. Its purpose is to "encourage a child who may be reluctant to tell a story" (para 12.19). A problem arises when it is sought to adduce a video tape made of the facilitative stage in evidence. The tape may contain questioning designed to pressure the child into disclosure of abuse. One criticism of this kind of interview is that it assumes that there is abuse to be disclosed and that therefore a child is denying to adults an experience of abuse that in fact occurred; it is not accepted that the child has no abuse to disclose. Thus even if the evidence is admitted, either by agreement or under the statutory exceptions to the hearsay rule, little weight will be attached to the video tape.

The professionals who conduct the facilitative stage of interviewing are child psychiatrists and psychologists. The Report states that "they are not likely to be interviewing more than a small number of children suspected of being abused, and seldom, if ever, at an initial interview" (para 12.12). However, it will be seen that the case law concerning video taped interviews with children in wardship and custody hearings concerns questioning by such professionals. In some cases the child is referred by a medical practitioner to the sexual abuse clinic at Great Ormond Street Hospital for Sick Children. Social workers and/or the police do not always interview the child before such a referral.

In *Re E (A Minor) (Child Abuse: Evidence)* (1987) and in *Re W (Minors) (Child Abuse: Evidence)* (1987), children were referred directly by paediatricians to the Great Ormond Street clinic. The holding of a formal interview is thus not an absolute pre-condition before the conduct of a facilitative one. A major difficulty in using video tapes of facilitative interviews as evidence in court is that techniques which were originally developed to provide therapy for abused children are now applied for diagnostic or disclosure purposes, to establish whether abuse occurred. Hence, as stated earlier, the style of questioning employed does not lend credence to the diagnosis made so far as courts of law are concerned.

5. The weight attached to video recorded interviews

In the cases in which judicial comment is made as to the weight to be attached to video recorded interviews with children thought to have been abused, the recordings have been admitted by agreement. The only issue for the judge therefore is the factual one of whether the recording tends to prove that abuse has occurred. The standard of proof looked for in these cases is the balance of probabilities, since they are civil matters. However, in *Avon County Council* v *G* (1988), it was suggested that the standard of proof where sexual abuse by a father is alleged might be higher than where abuse is alleged without reference to a particular perpetrator. Further, it was suggested that the concept of a standard of proof might be inappropriate in sexual abuse cases, since the very fact that an allegation of sexual abuse had been made by a child (particularly an older child) might indicate that a change of regime in relation to that child was desirable. Equally, it might be the case that:

> "a suspicion of sexual abuse or other wrong-doing, although incapable of formal proof, was such as to lead to the conclusion that it would be an unacceptable risk to the child's welfare to leave him in his previous environment." (per Mr Justice Sheldon)

The judicial criticisms made of the evidential value of recordings in the cases now discussed do not detract from the value of video tapes in assisting the court to determine whether abuse has taken place. It is the conduct of the interview, not the principle of video recording, which is so often criticised. Indeed in *Re M (A Minor) (Child Abuse: Evidence)* (1987), Mr Justice Latey stated that there were often cases where there was nothing more than a combination of alerting symptoms. In these cases no existing external evidence established that sexual abuse had occurred. In such cases:

> "There should always be a video recording. The reason is

> this: where there is a dispute whether there has or has not been abuse the court is anxious whether it should accept the *ipse dixit* of the interviewer or interviewers, however skilled and experienced. This is because the cases have shown that the precise questions, the oral answers (if there are any) and body movements, the vocal inflection and intonation may all play an important part in interpretation. Where there is a dispute there should be an opportunity for another expert in the field to form a view."

A second psychiatric opinion can therefore be obtained on the basis of the tape and the child is possibly spared the need for another interview. A video recording has the further advantage that the court can form its own opinion of the interview. However, it was stated by Mr Justice Waite in *Re W (Minors) (Child Abuse: Evidence)* (1987) that although a video tape was helpful to the court in that it enables the court to catch the context and flavour of the interview:

> "Recourse to a video tape recording can never be an acceptable substitute for the overall view which the court has to take of the evidence as a whole. In my view of the case, it has taken its place simply as part of the record of the interview, and as affording a means by which I am enabled in a general context to assess the probative value of the interview, alongside all other considerations presented by the evidence."

The criticisms of recorded interviews fall into two main categories. Firstly it is alleged that the questioning employed produces no valid finding of abuse in that the child is led into making allegations of sexual abuse by the questioner. Secondly, it is argued in relation to some recorded interviews that the child's responses do not necessarily imply a finding of abuse. In other words it is the interpretation of the interview which is challenged. Obviously these two issues are often intertwined.

(a) Leading and hypothetical questioning

In *Re N (Minors) (Child Abuse: Evidence)* (1987) criticism of the style of questioning adopted by a psychological social worker was made by a child psychiatrist (Dr Connell). Dr Connell stated that he had misgivings about the technique used at Great Ormond Street in cases of non-admitted sexual abuse. He stated:

> "I have doubts about the value of the technique. It has a place as a therapeutic tool, and in family dynamics, but where there is no admission of sexual abuse, I have grave hesitations about the scientific or clinical value of the technique."

He then made a specific criticism of the questioning in that case:

> "My view of the text is that the child said very little, if anything. Very strong pressure was brought to bear by Miss Tranter with leading questions. There was a technique when receiving a negative answer to assume that it was positive. To me it seemed that the tone of voice had a bias towards an answer which would confirm the presence of sexual abuse . . . In the face of two-choice questions the incriminating choice was always second and a child, not thinking very clearly, would choose the most recent suggestion."

The judge in this case found that it was unlikely that sexual abuse had taken place. He stated that considerable pressure had been brought to bear upon the child and he referred to the nine or ten occasions when the child had freely volunteered the information that no abuse had taken place. He stated:

> "I am bound to say, having seen the video recording, it may well be that too little attention was paid to the child's statements, made quite freely as I saw them, that nothing untoward had occurred as opposed to her statements in answer to direct questions under pressure that indecency had taken place." (per Swinton-Thomas J)

In *C* v *C (Child Abuse: Evidence)* (1987) a video recording had been made of an interview between the child in question and a consultant psychiatrist and a psychiatric social worker at Great Ormond Street. The recording had been erased before it could be produced to the court. A transcript of the interview was never taken and the consultant psychiatrist's notes were lost. Another consultant psychiatrist (Dr Zeitlin) saw the video tape before it had been erased. His report on the interview was considered by the court. It was his opinion that:

> "Throughout the interview there was heavy pressure from the interviewing adults on the child. If the child does not spontaneously demonstrate what is expected, then it is actively demonstrated to the child. The terms are fed to the child by the interviewers and the mother, and at one point the mother tells the child what to say. The dolls are positioned by the interviewers, and after an unsuccessful attempt to get a positive statement from the child a second attempt appears more successful. . . . The other doll is continually identified by the adults as "daddy" and never spontaneously by the child."

The issue in the case was whether the father should have access to the child on divorce. In fact access was agreed between the parents before the hearing. However, Mr Justice Hollis commented to the effect that he was not convinced that such diagnostic interviews were in the best interests of the child except possibly where sexual abuse had been proved. He stated that there should be no preliminary discussion of the allegations in front of the child concerned and that the complaining parent should never be present during the interview (as was the case in *C* v *C*). He then said:

> "Neither do I think that these anatomically explicit dolls should be used in a suggestive or leading way, though they may have their uses by people skilled in their use in helping to get at the truth. I was horrified to hear . . . that these dolls seem to have popped up all over the country, sometimes being used by people who are quite unqualified to use them. I hope that it will not happen any more."

Thus it can be seen that the value of the recorded interview as a piece of evidence is lost, if the style of the questioning used destroys the credibility of the child's testimony.

(b) The interpretation of the interview

In *Re G (Minors) (Child Abuse: Evidence)* (1987), the issue was again whether a father should be allowed access to his children. The mother alleged that he had sexually abused his daughter. A psychological social worker at Great Ormond Street held interviews with both son and daughter after which she concluded that both children had been abused. Sexually explicit dolls were utilised in the interview, which in fact took place before the practice of video taping was introduced. Mr Justice Ewbank commented that when he had last dealt with a case of this nature he had seen the video and was thus "able to compare what was actually said with the conclusions that were drawn from what was said." He made it clear that on that occasion his conclusions had been affected by the fact that the interview had been based upon a preconception that abuse had taken place. He had therefore differed from the conclusion reached by the psychological social worker. In *Re G*, evidence was also received from a consultant psychiatrist to the effect that conclusions drawn from the use of sexually explicit dolls were of no evidential validity. The psychiatrist had stated that the use of such dolls was:

> "about as valuable as producing in a fire-raising case concerning a child, model houses, a model fire engine, a can of petrol and a box of matches. He says that you could not draw any conclusions from a child who started a fire under those circumstances and by the same token ought not to draw any conclusions from anything the child does with the sexually explicit dolls."

Three principles concerning the inferences which may be drawn from a recorded interview emerge from this case. Firstly, the fact that a video tape of the interview exists allows the judge (and any other professional instructed in the case) to form his own conclusions, having seen the tape, as to whether the interview discloses sexual abuse. Secondly, the interviewing techniques used will be a relevant factor, so far as the judge is concerned, in reaching a conclusion as to whether abuse is disclosed. Thirdly, the inferences drawn from the interview are not based solely upon the verbal responses of the child. The physical actions of the child (particularly those demonstrating sexual activity in relation to the dolls provided for the purpose) are taken into account. Some child psychiatrists and social workers have greater faith than others in the validity of inferences to be drawn from the use of such dolls.

A difference of interpretation as to the physical actions of the child is illustrated by the case of *Re N (Minors) (Child Abuse)* (above). The gestures made by the child were interpreted by the interviewing psychological social worker as indicating that masturbation with the father had taken place. A child psychiatrist viewed the video recording and concluded that he did not think the gesture made by the child led to this conclusion. The judge stated:

> "There was some difference of view about that matter between those who had viewed the video, but I am bound to say my own impression, having seen it only once, which was less than counsel and others in the case, was that the movement made by IN with her finger would not normally be described as a masturbatory gesture."

Generally, the inferences drawn from a video tape are based on a combination of responses from the child. Verbal responses, gestures and the demeanour of the child (particularly on being confronted by anatomically correct dolls) can all be considered relevant in making a judgement as to sexual abuse. It can be seen from reported cases, however, that even amongst child psychiatrists there is considerable disagreement as to how an interview with a possibly abused child should be interpreted. The advantage of a video recording is that it allows another expert to form an opinion and thereby gives the court the benefit of a range of professional views upon which to base a decision.

6. The quality of the recordings

Although the Cleveland Report was essentially in favour of video recording interviews with children concerning possible sexual abuse, a caveat was made concerning the quality of the recording. If excellent quality and sound are not obtained, there is a danger of losing the "subtle nuances of interaction" (para 12.48 of the Report). It was stated that "The tapes which we viewed were in some instances difficult to follow and consequently not very helpful" (para 12.52). It is important therefore that good equipment is used and that it is used competently. However, on balance the Report concluded that "video recordings are a helpful step in the record of assessment of the child in appropriate circumstances, and with the necessary consents are in the interests of the child" (para 12.53).

Chapter 4

Discovery and privilege

1. Introduction

Discovery (which applies in civil proceedings only) is the disclosure by one party to another party of the existence of documents which are or have been in his custody. The documents must be relevant in that they tend to support or damage the party's case. The main purpose of discovery is to enable parties to evaluate the case in advance of trial and so to promote a settlement of the action. Discovery also effects a saving in costs in that evidence (particularly expert evidence) may be agreed in advance of the trial. The rules concerning the procedure for discovery are contained in Order 24 of the Rules of the Supreme Court and Order 14 of the County Court Rules. They are complex and outside the scope of this book. This chapter is concerned not with the detailed procedure of discovery, but with whether electronically recorded evidence can be the subject of such a process.

Privilege is the right to withhold information or inspection of certain documents from the parties to the action and the court. This right exists in limited situations in both civil and criminal proceedings. There are various categories of privilege, but the one which is discussed in this chapter is that of "public policy" privilege. This form of privilege applies equally in civil and criminal proceedings. In both kinds of proceeding the rationale for the privilege is that:

> "by reason of the character of the information or the relationship of the recipient of the information to the

> informant a more important public interest is served by protecting the information or the identity of the informant from disclosure in a court of law" (per Lord Denning in *D* v *NSPCC* (1978)).

Inevitably the application of such a principle involves a balancing exercise. On the one hand it is in the interests of justice that the court should have all the available information before it. On the other hand, to force disclosure in certain situations might lead to public loss of trust in and co-operation with the disclosing party (for example, in police forces or social services departments, when information is given in confidence). This chapter is concerned with the decisions that have been made in relation to three categories of professionals, all of whom use electronically recorded evidence in the course of their official duties. They are journalists, social workers/child psychologists and police officers.

Issues of discovery or privilege arise in civil proceedings when a litigant attempts to use electronically recorded evidence to establish his case. He might wish, for instance, in a civil action for assault, to rely upon a video tape of a public disturbance. Parents may seek to use video recordings made by social workers in custody or wardship disputes, or even as evidence when suing a social work department for negligence. The police may wish to see evidence recorded by doctors or social workers in order to substantiate a criminal prosecution for sexual abuse or to see a journalist's recording of a disturbance in order to substantiate charges of public disorder.

2. Discovery

A tape recording is a document discovery of which can be sought under Order 24 Rules of the Supreme Court. In the case of *Rex* v *Daye* (1908) it was held that the essential feature of a document was "the information thereby conveyed". This was reiterated in *Hill* v *R* (1945) where it was stated:

> "a document must be something which teaches you and from which you can learn something, ie. it must be something which affords information. . . . To constitute a

document, the form it takes seems to me to be immaterial." (per Humphreys J)

These cases were cited with approval in *Grant* v *Southwestern and County Properties* (1975) where discovery of a tape recorded conversation was sought by the defendants. The action involved an alleged breach of partnership agreement and the tape provided evidence of a telephone conversation which was relevant to the alleged terms of the partnership. The court held in favour of the defendants. The tapes were documents for the purposes of discovery and the "mere interposition of necessity of an instrument for deciphering the information cannot make any difference in principle." Thus, although the reading of a tape recording by the eye is impossible, it is still a document. The same principles apply to video tapes. The necessity of using a tape or video recorder to play back the information does not prevent it being the subject of an order for discovery.

In *Senior and Others* v *Holdsworth* (1975), the Court of Appeal held that the court had power to compel a witness to produce a film in court by the issue of a summons *duces tecum* and also had power to order the witness to exhibit the film, that is, provide the apparatus for showing it. Lord Justices Orr and Scarman considered that in the county court this could be achieved (providing that any expense incurred was treated as part of the costs of the action) either under Order 13 rule 3 of the County Court Rules, or under its inherent discretion. Lord Denning stated that in the High Court there was an inherent discretion to make an order for the production and playing of tape recordings and for the production and showing of film. He considered that the county court could adopt that jurisdiction under s 103 County Courts Act 1959, which states that in any case not expressly provided for by the Act itself, the county court may adopt the general principles of practice of the High Court.

In *Senior* v *Holdsworth*, Independent Television News Limited had made films of a pop music festival that was held in Windsor Great Park. On the last day of the festival there were disorders in which the police intervened. The plaintiffs were suing the Chief Constable for assaults allegedly committed during the disturbances. One of the plaintiffs issued a summons to the producer of ITN, requiring him to attend trial and to bring with him "all film and negative taken of the breakup of the festival" together with the equipment to show the film and video. ITN objected to producing untransmitted film on the basis that to do so would conflict with their duties under the Independent Broadcasting Act 1973. Section 4(1)(b) of this Act requires ITN to satisfy itself that all news is presented with due accuracy and impartiality. They argued that the transmitted film had been selected on that basis and therefore that the rest of the film ought not to be disclosed. They also argued that to depart from a general policy of not producing untransmitted film would put themselves and their camera crew in a difficult (and possibly dangerous) position and could, in some circumstances, involve a disclosure of confidential sources. Rejecting these arguments, the court held that:

> "an incident which may properly have been omitted from the transmitted film, for instance because it may produce a false impression of the overall scene, may be of great importance for the purposes of a criminal or civil case or a public enquiry . . . and it would be in no way inconsistent with ITN's statutory duty of impartiality that untransmitted film of such an incident should be disclosed for the purpose of proceedings." (per Orr LJ)

However, the court stated that although the issue of a summons *duces tecum* was an administrative not a judicial act and therefore one which the registrar did not have jurisdiction to refuse, the court had a discretion to set aside a summons to produce documents of journalists and broadcasters. It could do so where the material was not otherwise privileged from production, on the ground that it was oppressive to require the whole film to be shown. Further, the applicant for the summons should give as clear information as possible as to the time and nature of the incident in question.

The principle of oppression should logically apply whenever discovery of electronically recorded evidence is sought, whatever the profession of the witness who made the recording. However, such an issue is most likely to apply in proceedings where the evidence sought has been recorded by a journalist rather than by social workers, psychologists or the police. The reason is that public policy privilege is far more likely to apply in relation to the latter three professions and therefore to preclude inspection of electronically recorded material on discovery. Privilege is discussed below. Another reason for the less widespread applicability of discovery to recordings made by those working with children is that such an order will rarely be made in wardship or custody proceedings. It was stated in *Re D (Infants)* (1970) that such an order should only be made in wardship or custody cases in exceptional circumstances. In that case (a wardship hearing) the court refused to order the disclosure of case records kept by the county council, even though the local authority was a party to the proceedings.

The next part of this chapter deals with how a claim for discovery can be defeated by a claim that the recordings are privileged material.

3. Privilege in civil proceedings

(a) Journalists

As stated above, a claim of privilege against discovery of journalistic material is unlikely to be upheld. The claim is usually based upon the fact that the information forming the journalistic material has been received and is held in confidence. The applicability of privilege was discussed in *British Steel Corporation* v *Granada Television* (1980). The House of Lords held that there was no immunity based on public interest protecting journalists from disclosing their sources of information when such disclosure was necessary in the interests of justice. Lord Wilberforce stated:

> "I start with the proposition that the media of information, and journalists who write or contribute for them, have no immunity based on public interest which protects them from that obligation to disclose in a court of law their sources of information, when such disclosure is necessary in the interests of justice . . . no such claim has ever been allowed in our courts and such attempts as have been made to assert immunity have failed."

Lord Fraser considered that public interest in the administration of justice required confidential information to be disclosed. This prevailed over the public interest of preserving confidentiality. There was an acknowledgement, however, that the courts would not force a breach of confidentiality where it was not essential or where the information could be obtained from another source. Ironically, it seems that electronic recordings made by journalists may enjoy a greater degree of protection from production in criminal proceedings than in civil proceedings. This is the result of the provisions in PACE concerning excluded material and special procedure material, which are considered later in this chapter (see page 64).

(b) Social workers, psychologists, psychiatrists

In *Re D (Infants)* (1970) the court held that case records compiled and kept by the local authority pursuant to the regulations controlling the boarding out of children were privileged from disclosure because: "these records must not be kept by people looking over their shoulders in case they should be attacked for some opinion which they feel it their duty to express." (per Harman LJ)

Public policy therefore required that they should remain confidential. In the leading case of *D* v *NSPCC* (1978), a mother brought an action against the NSPCC for damages for personal injury alleged to have resulted from the Society's negligent investigation of a complaint. She alleged that the manner in which the investigation had been conducted had caused her severe and continuing shock. The NSPCC objected to producing any documents that might reveal the identity of the complainant on the ground that the preservation of confidence was in the public interest. The House of Lords (reversing the Court of Appeal decision) upheld the claim of the NSPCC against discovery. Two of the judges (Lords Hailsham and Diplock) based their decision on the narrow ground of the immunity afforded to police informants. Lord Hailsham stated:

> "Once, however, it is accepted that information given to the police in the instant case would have been protected, it becomes . . . manifestly absurd that it should not be accorded equally to the same information if given by the

same informant to the local authority . . . or to the appellant society, to whom according to the undisputed evidence ordinary informants more readily resort."

Lord Diplock upheld a claim of privilege on this ground, but he asserted that confidentiality of itself did not provide a ground for non-disclosure. However, Lord Edmund-Davies considered the wider issues of public policy involving confidential relationships. He concluded that:

> "In civil proceedings the judge has no discretion, simply because what is contemplated is the disclosure of information which has passed between persons in a confidential relationship (other than that of lawyer and client) to direct a party to that relationship that he need not disclose that information . . . but where (1) a confidential relationship exists . . . and (2) disclosure would be in breach of some ethical or social value involving the public interest, the court has a discretion to uphold a refusal to disclose relevant evidence provided it considers that, on balance, the public interest would be better served by excluding such evidence."

Lord Edmund-Davies considered that the mere fact that the information is communicated in confidence does not lead to a claim of privilege, but where the subject matter is of public interest, the additional fact that to breach confidentiality would endanger that interest "will in most (if not all cases) probably lead to the conclusion that disclosure should be withheld."

The wider approach taken in *D* v *NSPCC* was subsequently relied upon in *Gaskin* v *Liverpool City Council* (1980). The prospective plaintiff (who had been in the care of the local authority for almost his entire minority) claimed to be suffering from severe psychological injuries and anxiety neurosis which he attributed to the authority's negligence or breach of duty whilst he was in their care.

He applied for production and disclosure of all case notes and records made upon him in respect of his period in care. The Court of Appeal (upholding the decision of the judges at first instance) held that the public interest in the proper functioning of the child care service required that confidentiality of the documents should be preserved. Lord Denning drew a parallel between "child care privilege" and legal professional privilege. He cited both *Re D (Infants)* and *D* v *NSPCC* in support of this proposition. The gradual emergence of a privilege in respect of confidential social work records has thus taken place within the framework of public policy privilege.

This does not mean, however, that video recordings made by social workers are automatically privileged from discovery. In order for a claim of privilege to arise, the recording must be categorised as a document, that is, it must be documentary not direct evidence (see Chapters 1 and 2). In *Bolton Metropolitan Borough Council* v *W* (1988) two children were made wards of court and committed to the care of the local authority. The mother applied for access, and interim access was granted at the discretion of the local authority. The access visits were video taped by social workers. The authority then decided to terminate access altogether on the basis that it was damaging to the children. Counsel for the mother sought discovery of the video recordings so that they could be seen by an expert witness and be made available to the court at the hearing. The local authority objected to producing the recordings on the basis that they were privileged. Judge Hardy held that the recordings were of an entirely different nature from reports and records prepared by social workers in the course of their duties. They were simply "audible and visible records of events in which the persons in dispute played a part in producing." Thus the recordings were direct evidence of the visits between mother and child. They recorded rather than created information and could not be the subject of a privilege claim. Interviews between social worker and child, held to establish abuse, will probably be documentary evidence, however, because the truth of the child's assertions is likely to be in issue (see Chapter 2).

Psychologists and child psychiatrists should be entitled to claim privilege on the same basis as a social worker. However, in *Campbell* v *Tameside Metropolitan Borough Council* (1982) it was held that the reports of teachers, psychologists and psychiatrists were not privileged. The reports concerned an eleven year old boy who had violently assaulted a teacher in the classroom. The documents were held to be of crucial significance on issues as to whether the defendants knew or ought to have known that the boy was of a violent disposition and should not have attended the plaintiff's class. Lord Denning stated that:

> "Reports of doctors and nurses are, of course, confidential; but they must always be disclosed: subject to the safeguard that they are used only in connection with the instant case and for no other purpose."

Yet Lord Denning considered that reports of "children's officers" were privileged "as a class" rather than because of their actual contents. It is difficult to understand why a video recorded interview made by a social worker should be privileged and yet one made by a child psychiatrist would not be. It is suggested that a safer criterion than the professional label of the interviewer would be the purpose of the application for discovery.

In *Gaskin* v *Liverpool City Council*, the court considered that the solicitors for the potential plaintiff were "fishing" in an attempt to discover a cause of action. Lord Denning stated that the solicitors for the plaintiff should not be allowed to "roam through the whole of this young man's file to see if in some way or another they can find a case". In *Campbell* v *Tameside Metropolitan Borough Council* (1982), the court treated the application as a straightforward claim for medical negligence. No distinction was made between the application in that case and an application made by a plaintiff suing a hospital authority for negligence. It would therefore seem that if (for instance) a parent is suing a hospital authority for medical negligence on the basis that a psychiatrist or paediatrician has wrongly made a diagnosis of sexual abuse, no claim of privilege would lie to prevent discovery of any video tapes made of conversations between doctor and child. If, however, a claim of negligence in diagnosis is part of a wider general claim of negligence concerning the welfare agencies' treatment of parents and child, it is suggested that the claim of privilege would possibly lie, even though the recording was made by a psychologist rather than a social worker.

(c) The police

Electronic recordings in the possession of the police may be of crucial importance in establishing a claim for personal injury or false imprisonment against the relevant Police Commissioner. It might, for instance, be alleged that one or more members of a force assaulted the plaintiff whilst attempting to control a public demonstration, the demonstration having been recorded on video tape by means of cameras (sited in public areas) linked to police headquarters. The police might then seek to argue that the recordings are privileged within the general category of public privilege. In *Peach* v *Commissioner of Police of the Metropolis* (1986) a demonstrator died after being struck upon the head by an unidentified police officer. Immediately after his death, the police began an investigation and obtained answers to questionnaires and statements from witnesses. The Commissioner objected to producing these documents, claiming that they were privileged on the grounds of public interest. The Court of Appeal made a distinction between evidence taken solely for the purpose of an inquiry into police conduct and that taken for other purposes. Privilege applied in the former situation. It did not apply, however, where the evidence was taken (as in the instant case) with the dominant purpose of ascertaining how the deceased died. Since recorded evidence of a scene of disorder will not be taken for the purpose of a police inquiry, it seems unlikely that any claim of privilege will be sustainable in a subsequent civil action against the police.

4. Disclosure in wardship cases

Quite independently of any issue of privilege, PACE provides that confidential material in the possession of social workers, psychologists and doctors can only be seized by order of the court. The relevant provisions are considered in section 5 below. Where the child is already a ward of court, however, the police may wish to see evidence tendered at a wardship hearing in order to substantiate a prosecution against a parent or other person for an offence committed against the ward. In *Re S (Minors) (Wardship: Police Investigation)* (1987), four wards (who were suspected of being sexually abused) were committed to the care of the local authority. The authority was granted leave to take the wards to the clinic at Great Ormond Street Hospital. The clinic considered that some, if not all, the wards had been sexually abused. The police began an investigation into whether criminal proceedings should be brought against the cohabitee of the wards' mother. The Commissioner of Police sought leave of the court to permit disclosure to the police of the records and video recordings made by the clinic, and also leave to further interview the wards and to inspect the case records of the local authority.

The following principles emerge from the judgment in that case:

(i) notwithstanding that the wards have been committed to the care and control of the local authority, the court retains a duty to protect the wards until the discharge of wardship;

(ii) whether the police should see medical records, video recordings etc. for the purpose of a criminal investigation is a matter for the judge exercising wardship jurisdiction, from whom directions should be sought;

(iii) the court has unfettered discretion to grant leave for disclosure. The court will balance the interests of the wards against the public interest requiring that the police should not be obstructed in pursuing a criminal investigation.

In the instant case, leave was given to disclose the relevant material and to further interview the wards. Even though the children might be subjected to further stress and might be called to give evidence in criminal proceedings, the public interest, requiring the court to protect society from the perpetration of crime, prevailed. It was said that it would only be "in exceptional circumstances" that the interests of the individual ward would prevail. It would seem from the decisions of *In Re F (A Minor) and Others* (1988) that exactly the same balancing exercise will be undertaken by a wardship judge where the police are seeking disclosure of the evidence submitted at the wardship hearing itself.

It is to be noted that where criminal charges have been laid in cases of sexual abuse, before the children in issue are made wards of court, it would be "constitutionally improper" for the wardship court to intervene in the conduct of the criminal trial (see *In Re K (Minors) (Wardship: Criminal*

Proceedings) (1987)). Thus the children cannot be protected from giving evidence other than by means of the use of video links to avoid confrontation with the accused.

5. Disclosure to the police of evidence held in confidence

Police powers of search and seizure relating to electronically recorded evidence are substantially modified where the evidence sought is held in confidence. The provisions of The Police and Criminal Evidence Act 1984 ("PACE") now discussed, apply to journalists and to social workers and doctors. The majority of electronically recorded evidence held by these professionals will fall within the definition of either "excluded material" or "special procedure material". An order of the court is necessary before production of such material can be compelled.

(a) Journalists

Section 11 of PACE defines "excluded material" as including "journalistic material which a person holds in confidence" and which consists of documents or records other than documents. Tapes and video tapes clearly fall within the definition of document. Section 118(1) of PACE adopts the definition of "document" given in the Civil Evidence Act 1968 (see page 19). Section 13(1) defines "journalistic material" as material in the possession of a person who acquired or created it for the purposes of journalism. It is the purpose for which the material is held, not the status of the person holding it, that is relevant. Thus an amateur photographer using a video camera to record a robbery could argue that he held journalistic material if he intended that the film should be used subsequently in a news broadcast. It is unlikely that such material would be held in confidence, however, and thus it would not be excluded material, but it could be "special procedure" material (see page 65 *et seq*).

The police may obtain excluded material in two ways. The first way is to obtain the consent in writing of the person entitled to grant entry to the premises which it is intended to search for material. The officer in charge of the search must state the purpose of the search and inform the person concerned that he is not obliged to consent and that anything seized may be produced in evidence (para 4, Code B of Codes of Practice under PACE). Where such consent to a search is forthcoming, it appears that by virtue of s 19 PACE, a constable may seize anything on the premises if he has reasonable grounds to believe it is evidence in relation to an offence. It may be the offence which he is investigating "or any other offence". It must be necessary to seize the evidence in order to prevent it being concealed, lost or destroyed.

The second method of obtaining excluded material is for the police to apply to a circuit judge for a warrant under Sch 1 of PACE. The provisions of Sch 1 are somewhat complex. They apply to the recorded interviews of social workers and psychiatrists equally (see page 68). The police may not obtain a warrant from a magistrate. They must satisfy a circuit judge that:

(i) there are reasonable grounds for believing that there is material which consists of excluded material on the premises specified in the application; and

(ii) if it were not excluded material, a warrant could have been issued to authorise a search of the premises (s 9(2) PACE); and

(iii) the issue of such a warrant would have been appropriate.

These conditions are referred to as the "second set of access conditions" and they apply equally to special procedure material (below). If the conditions are satisfied, the judge can make an order that the material be produced to a constable or that a constable be given access to it. The order must be complied with within seven days or such longer period as the order may specify. Failure to comply with a production order will entitle the police to apply for a warrant under Sch 1 para 12. Additionally the possessor of the material may be dealt with for contempt (para 15).

Non-confidential journalistic material will be "special procedure" material. Section 14(1)(b) of PACE defines special procedure material as including "journalistic material other than excluded material". The police may obtain special procedure material by consent (see above) or under Sch 1 of PACE. The police must prove that one of two sets of access conditions is satisfied. The second set of conditions replicates those for access to excluded material. Identical provisions apply as to the making of production orders and the issue of warrants. The first set of access conditions differs in that it applies where, before PACE, the police could not have obtained a warrant and so cannot now do so. The judge must be satisfied that:

(i) there are reasonable grounds for believing that:
- a serious arrestable offence has been committed, and
- there is material which consists of or includes special procedure material (but not excluded material) on the premises specified in the application, and
- the material is likely to be of substantial value to the investigation and
- the material is likely to be relevant evidence;

(ii) other methods of obtaining the material have been tried without success or would appear bound to fail; and

(iii) it is in the public interest that the material should be produced or access given.

In making a decision as to whether it is in the public interest to order production of the material, the judge will consider the benefit likely to accrue to the investigation if the material is obtained and the circumstances in which the person in possession holds the relevant material.

In *R* v *Bristol Crown Court ex parte Bristol Press and Picture Agency* (1987) the High Court considered the operation of the above provisions with regard to special procedure material. The case concerned photographs taken during violent disturbances in the St Paul's district of Bristol. It could equally well have concerned pictures taken by means of a video camera. The applicants were an agency providing photographs and other journalistic material for the local and national press. One of their directors and another member of staff were present during the disturbances and took photographs. The police believed that the photographs would assist them in identifying the persons who committed offences, by showing details of offences in respect of which no charges had yet been made and, perhaps, in showing that some of those charged or suspected were in fact not guilty. With the exception of those photographs which had already appeared in the press, the applicants refused to comply with police requests to see the photographs. It was agreed that the photographs were special procedure material (they were not confidential) and the issue was whether the photographs were likely to be of "substantial value to the investigation" within Sch 1 of PACE. It was argued for the applicants that the term "investigation" must be related to some particular criminal offence or offences and that a whole series of possible disturbances was too wide to come within the Schedule. It was further argued that the test of substantial value could not be satisfied without knowledge of whether the photographs showed anything of significance.

The High Court approved the decision of the judge at first instance and held that conditions in Sch 1 were satisfied. It cited with approval the first instance judgment to the effect that:

> "It is well known that in the case of fast moving crimes such as riots and affrays, particularly where the victims may be the subject of attack by several assailants, the identification of those involved in the offence is a matter of great difficulty . . . A photograph which helps to identify an offender and particularly a series of photographs of the same incident which may help to show that a gesture or movement is in fact a blow and not capable of innocent explanation, may be of great value to the investigation."

Thus a video tape of the incident would, under the above criteria, prove an invaluable aid to the police in formulating charges as a consequence of a situation of public disorder and would meet the requirements of PACE. The fact that the whole episode (rather than specific incidents of criminality) has been recorded is no bar to the making of a production order. It was accepted that journalists would take pictures of assaults and acts of criminal damage "for the very good reason that these are newsworthy" rather than "confining their attentions to groups of docile policemen or law-abiding citizens returning from Bingo".

The issue of "public interest" within Sch 1 was also discussed in this case. It was said that the court must undertake a balancing exercise between the public interest in the investigation of crime and the public interest in the press being free to report and to photograph as much as they can of what is going on in deprived areas of cities. The applicants expressed concern that the press would not be able to go about their job in safety if production of journalistic material were to be ordered in this kind of situation. The High Court considered that the judge at first instance had applied the right test and had taken account of all relevant considerations in reaching his decision. He had been right to order production. The public interest "that those guilty of crime and particularly of serious crime involving widespread public disorder, should be brought to justice" prevailed. This approach has been endorsed recently in the case of *Re an Application under section 9 of the Police and Criminal Evidence Act 1984* (1988) where it was stated that it was in the public interest to order the production of special procedure material (unpublished films and photographs) where this would help criminal investigation and not undermine freedom of the press.

(b) Social workers, psychologists, psychiatrists

Video recordings made by social workers, psychologists or psychiatrists will be excluded material within PACE. Section 11(1)(a) defines excluded material as including:

> "personal records which a person has acquired or created in the course of any trade, business, profession or other occupation or for the purposes of any paid or unpaid office and which he holds in confidence".

Section 12 defines "personal records" as "documentary and other records concerning an individual who can be identified from them". The documentary material must relate to one of the following matters:

(i) the individual's physical or mental health;

(ii) spiritual counselling or assistance to be given to the individual; or

(iii) counselling or assistance given or to be given to the individual for the purpose of his personal welfare. The counselling may be given by any voluntary organisation or by any individual who by reason of his office or occupation has responsibilities for the personal welfare of the subject, or by reason of a court order has responsibilities for his supervision.

Thus the "personal record" element is clearly satisfied in any interview recorded by professionals dealing with children and their families in cases of suspected or proven child abuse. It would also apply to a tape recording made by a psychiatrist of a conversation with a patient in which the patient revealed that he or she had committed an offence. The appropriate procedures for obtaining this material, in the absence of consent, have already been outlined in connection with journalistic material, above. It is perhaps worth stating that if an interview, recorded by a social worker or doctor, were not considered to be a personal record for any reason, then the material would nevertheless be special procedure material within s 14 of PACE. This section defines special procedure material as including material in the possession of a person who acquired or created it in the course of any "trade, business, profession or other occupation or for the purpose of any paid or unpaid office" and who holds it "subject to an express or implied undertaking to hold it in confidence".

6. Public policy privilege claims by the police

The police may claim immunity from disclosing the sources of their information in criminal proceedings under the general heading of public policy privilege. The privilege has long been recognised as protecting the anonymity of police informants: *Marks* v *Beyfus* (1890). The courts have only sanctioned an invasion of this privilege where knowledge of the identity of the informer is relevant to establish the innocence of the defendant or otherwise to prevent a miscarriage of justice: *R* v *Hallett* (1986).

The possibility that the privilege might now extend to police methods and techniques generally was recognised in *R* v *Brown, R* v *Daley* (1988). In that case the judge at first instance had decided that the prosecution could withhold information known to the police on the ground of public interest. The information in the case related to the colour, make and model of an unmarked police car that had allegedly been used in a surveillance operation. The appellants contended that they had been "fitted up" by the police and that the surveillance had in fact proved abortive. On the facts of the case, the appeal was upheld. The information should not have been withheld. However, although no authority had been referred to the court to support the contention that the making public of police methods or techniques was a public policy ground to exclude evidence, their Lordships did not rule out the possibility that the advent of sophisticated methods of criminal investigation might lead, in some cases, to a successful claim of public interest immunity, thereby justifying the exclusion of evidence of police surveillance. It was stated, however, that if and when such arguments were raised, the following procedure should be adopted. The Crown Prosecution Service must ensure that counsel is properly instructed to make the application and can identify with precision the evidence sought to be excluded and the reasons for its exclusion. The judge must be given as much information as possible. The application must be supported by the independent evidence of senior officers and not by the instructions of the junior officer in charge of the case. Thus some independent evidence must be produced to the court to support an argument of public interest immunity if the police are to succeed in withholding evidence of police methods. It is possible, therefore, that the police might sometimes succeed, in criminal proceedings, in withholding electronically recorded evidence such as tapes of conversations with informers or the fact that a video tape has been made of a surveillance operation.

Chapter 5

Privacy and electronic surveillance

1. The current use of video cameras

Surveillance by video cameras as a method of crime control is now commonplace; reported crime has reduced dramatically in areas covered by closed circuit television. The surveillance may be conducted by a private organisation or by the police. Banks, building societies and shops are equipped with video cameras to protect private premises to which the public have access. Private organisations are also responsible for the use of video cameras in shopping precincts and football grounds. The police use video cameras for surveillance in town centres and on public roads, that is, in public places. Wolverhampton is the first town in the country where the police employ video cameras to effect surveillance of the major part of the town centre. Ideally the mere presence of the strategically sited cameras will assist in the prevention of crime. However, the cameras are linked to the control room of a police station which houses video monitors and printers. A recording made of criminal activity will give a basis for arrest and will provide evidence in court, should the alleged offender plead not guilty. The generalised use of video cameras to "protect town centres from drunken violence and football hooligans" was discussed at the 1988 autumn conference of the Association of Chief Police Officers (The Times , 6 October).

The use of video cameras by motorway patrols is now usual practice. In road traffic cases, the video film may show the alleged offender committing the alleged offence, or may simply record for the benefit of the court the scene of the crime (see *R* v *Thomas*, page 4). The use of video cameras to deter and detect criminals is therefore not confined to the police, and the multiplicity of systems used means that many tapes have to be rendered "compatible" with the playback equipment in court. There is as yet no code of practice governing such a procedure. In all the above situations, however, whether surveillance is of public or private areas, the video camera is not used to photograph a specific individual identified in advance. This can clearly be distinguished from the recording of interviews (between social workers and children, for example) where the subject of the recording is predetermined. The objections to the use of video cameras on the ground that personal liberties are being infringed centre around random recording in public places. So far as the law of tort is concerned, however, there is no right to "be let alone". There is no tort involving breach of privacy *per se*.

2. English common law

The common law cases which involve the right to be let alone also involve the commission of some tort which is recognised as giving a cause of action. The old case of *Johnson* v *Wyatt* (1863) illustrates this principle. It was stated that no remedy could be granted to a householder to prevent the erection of a building which would overlook his own and destroy his privacy. Sometimes, however, the infringement of privacy coincides with the commission of other torts. These are trespass, nuisance, defamation, breach of copyright and breach of confidence. This last tort has potential for the widest application, but, ironically, it is more likely to assist the sexually abused child who is unaware that his or her revelations are being recorded, than the aggrieved motorist or football supporter (see page 74).

(a) Trespass and nuisance

Both trespass and nuisance require that the plaintiff has an interest in real property which is being infringed: *Malone* v *Laskey* (1907). In the case of *Bernstein* v *Skyviews* (1978) it was established that an owner's rights to prevent aerial photography of his premises were limited to preventing any intrusion into the airspace above his land. A land owner's airspace is essentially that space which is necessary for the ordinary use and enjoyment of the land and the structures upon it. Thus an action in trespass or nuisance would depend not on the fact that a photograph had been taken, but on the height from which it had been taken. Lord Griffiths stated that there was:

> "no principle of law or authority that would entitle Lord Bernstein to prevent someone taking a photograph of his property for an innocent purpose, provided they did not commit some other tort such as trespass or nuisance in doing so."

No tort of trespass would be committed in photographing a person in a public place or on a public road. Even if a video camera is specifically aimed at the house or business premises of an individual, no tort of trespass will arise if there is no physical interference with enjoyment of the premises. It is just conceivable that human observation of premises might amount to a nuisance, even if no element of trespass is involved. In *J Lyons and Son* v *Wilkins* (1899) it was thought possible that acts of "watching and besetting" were acts "themselves unlawful at common law". Lord Justice Chitty considered that: "every annoyance is not a nuisance; the annoyance must be of a serious character and of such a degree as to interfere with the ordinary comforts of life."

It is extremely unlikely that electronic surveillance would amount to a nuisance. It is unlikely to be an annoyance which interferes with the ordinary comforts of life of the observee. In most instances the observee will be unaware that observance is taking place. In any event, the surveillance will not be of the random kind employed in places to which the public have access. The tort of nuisance requires that the interference relates to rights in property.

(b) Defamation

A possible cause of action might arise through the law of defamation. A newspaper might, for instance, publish photographs taken with a video camera, in reporting on a court case where the video film was adduced in evidence. A person depicted might claim that the photographs defamed him in some way, that is, that the pictures convey an implication defaming him. Such an implication could arise, for instance, where an individual is photographed amidst a crowd of people who are committing public order offences. However, justification—a defence based on the truth of the published matter—would almost certainly provide a defence to such a claim. It was stated in *McPherson* v *Daniels* (1829) that "the law will not permit a man to recover damages in respect of an injury to a character which he does not or ought not to possess". Alternatively, the use of video film in the investigation of crime and in judicial proceedings would be protected by defences of qualified and absolute privilege respectively.

(c) Breach of copyright

Breach of copyright and/or contract might involve, incidentally, an invasion of privacy. In *Williams* v *Settle* (1960) the defendant (a professional photographer) was commissioned to take photographs of the plaintiff's wedding. The copyright in the photographs vested in the plaintiff. Two years later, the father of the plaintiff's wife was murdered. The defendant, without authority, sold certain of the photographs to representatives of the press. One of the photographs was published prominently in two national newspapers. The plaintiff succeeded in an action claiming damages for breach of copyright in the photographs. The recording of individuals as part of police surveillance or even the recording of individuals for interview purposes involves no breach of copyright, however.

(d) Breach of confidence

The classic case recognising breach of confidence as a tort is *Seager* v *Copydex Ltd* (1967). The case involved breach of a commercial confidence, even though conscious plagiarism was not in issue. It has recently been established that personal as opposed to commercial information can be the subject of a breach of confidence action. The case of *Stephens* v *Avery* (1988) involved the publication of an article in a newspaper concerning the sexual proclivities of the plaintiff. The plaintiff was alleged to have had a lesbian relationship with a married woman. The woman had been killed by her husband, as a consequence, it was alleged, of this relationship. The plaintiff claimed that she had imparted information concerning her sexual relationship to a friend expressly in confidence. It was accepted that the facts published were substantially correct. It was held that a cause of action for breach of confidence could exist even where the parties were not bound by an enforceable contract or a pre-existing relationship such as that of doctor/patient or employer/employee. The defendant's application to strike out the statement of claim was rejected. The Vice-Chancellor stated that three requirements had to be satisfied before the court could protect the information as being legally confidential. The information must have the necessary quality of confidence about it. It must have been imparted in circumstances importing an obligation of confidence, and it must have been used in an unauthorised way to the detriment of the party communicating it.

A pre-existing relationship of confidence between the parties must exist (even if only based upon friendship) before the above precepts can apply. No such confidential relationship is likely to intrude into the anonymous world of the remote-controlled video camera. It might, however, be an ingredient of social worker/client relationships. The Cleveland Report (see Chapter 3) was concerned that "problems may arise over the issue of consents and confidentiality in notes and video-recordings of interviews with children" (para 12.65). It was pointed out that in cases of alleged sexual abuse, complicated questions of confidentiality inevitably arise because of the conflict between professional ethics and the public interest in the detection of child sexual abuse. The Report stated that "much depends on who is the patient and to whom confidentiality is extended". It was recognised, however, that parents would need to appreciate that, in the interests of the child, information would need to be shared with professionals from many disciplines. The professional therefore has a duty to alert the family to the fact that video recordings of interviews may well be information that will be shared. The Report endorsed the view of the Children's Legal Centre that:

> "the use of sound or video recording equipment, two way mirrors, photography etc. should in every case be subject

to the specific consent of those subjected to the techniques, following a full explanation of the court's powers to view or hear recordings and a full explanation of the uses to which recordings may be put." (para 12.66).

It was also stated, however, that this procedure should apply to those children who were of an age and understanding to comprehend the explanation (para 12.67). No guidelines are given as to the age at which a child might be considered old enough to give an informed consent. It is yet to be seen whether the use of revelations by a child, as a basis for reception of that child into care and/or the basis of a criminal prosecution against either parent, could be an unauthorised user of confidential information within *Stephens* v *Avery*. Undoubtedly the professionals concerned in sharing the relevant information would argue that no detriment resulted to the party making the revelations (the child). A child who had been removed from his or her natural parent(s) as a consequence might well take a different view. The Report accepted that there was no easy answer to the problem of confidentiality where there was an obvious need to protect children against the inherently secret problem of family sexual abuse. At the very least, the practice of misleading a child into believing that a video recording will not be shown to outsiders, to parents or to the court, should be abandoned in favour of a more honest approach. It is acknowledged that this may deter some children from disclosing abuse but the child should be entitled to know the consequences involved in advance of making such disclosures. However, it is not the disclosure of sexual abuse on video tape that has produced protests as to the infringement of civil liberties. As stated earlier, most objections concern video surveillance of places to which the public have access. No argument as to breach of confidence can assist in these situations.

3. The Interception of Communications Act 1985

It should be noted that whilst there is no general constitutional restriction upon taping conversations and actions, the Interception of Communications Act 1985 puts some restrictions on telephone tapping (though, as will be seen, the scope of the remedy afforded by this statute is carefully defined). The statute was enacted as a consequence of an appeal by a British subject to the European Court of Human Rights. The appeal was against the decision of the Vice-Chancellor in the case of *Malone* v *Metropolitan Police Commissioner* (1979). Criminal proceedings had been brought against Malone and, during the course of those proceedings, it had become clear that his telephone had been tapped by the police. Malone then brought an action against the Police Commissioner claiming that the tapping of his telephone without his consent was unlawful (even if done pursuant to the Home Secretary's warrant). The argument was raised by Malone that the tapping was a breach of those rights of privacy, property and confidentiality which hc had in his telephone conversations and that the tapping violated the European Convention for the Protection of Human Rights. Article 8 of the Convention provides:

> "(1) Everyone has the right to respect for his private and family life, his home and his correspondence. (2) There shall be no interference by a public authority with the exercise of this right except such as is in accordance with the law and is necessary in a democratic society in the interests of national security, public safety or the economic well-being of the country, for the prevention of disorder or crime, for the protection of health or morals, or for the protection of the rights and freedom of others."

The Vice-Chancellor rejected Malone's claim on the basis that art 8 did not confer a direct right on the plaintiff to obtain a declaration on the matter in issue. He held that the Convention was not part of English law and therefore not justiciable. Mr Malone then took his case to the European Commission on Human Rights, and the Government meanwhile introduced legislation to bring United Kingdom law in line with the European Convention. The result was the Interception of Communications Act 1985. The Act followed the recommendations of the *Royal Commission on Criminal Procedure* (Cmnd 8092 paras 3.53–3.60) which stated that "the use of surveillance devices by the police (including the interception of letters and telephone communications) should be regulated by statute" (para 3.57). The Commission did not make more than a schematic description of the system of control which they desired. But it was stated that it would be necessary:

> "in devising a new system to take account of the findings of the European Court in the case of *Malone*, in which it has been alleged that the present controls over telephone tapping fall short of the requirements of article 8 of the European Convention for the Protection of Human Rights and Fundamental Freedoms." (para 3.60)

Section 1 of the Act creates a general offence of unlawful interception. The interception will be unlawful unless it is done either in obedience to a warrant issued by the Secretary of State or unless the interceptor has reasonable grounds to believe that the person to whom or the person by whom the communication is sent has consented to the interception. A warrant may be issued under s 2(2):

(i) in the interests of national security; or
(ii) for the purpose of preventing or detecting serious crime; or
(iii) for safeguarding the economic well-being of the United Kingdom.

The warrant authorises the interception of communications to or from a particular person or "particular set of premises" at a named address (s 3(1) of the Act). By s 3(2), where a communication is sent or received outside the British Islands, the warrant need only describe the *type* of communication. Where the communication is to or from an address in the British Islands, however, such a warrant may only be issued for the prevention of terrorism, and the period of interception may not exceed three months (s 3(3)). The warrant must be issued by the Secretary of State (the Home Secretary where a suspected crime is the basis of the interception) or, in an urgent case, by an Assistant Under Secretary of State (s 4(1)).

The issue of a warrant for the purpose of preventing or detecting serious crime is the ground relevant to police investigation. Section 10(3) of the Act provides that a crime is a serious crime if:

"(a) it involves the use of violence, results in substantial financial gain or is conducted by a large number of persons in pursuit of a common purpose; or
(b) the offence or one of the offences is an offence for

> which a person who has attained the age of 21 and has no previous convictions could reasonably be expected to be sentenced to imprisonment for a term of three years or more."

In any event, a tap should only be used where the information which it is considered necessary to acquire could not reasonably be acquired by other means (s 2(3)).

It is to be noted that even if unlawful tapping is believed to have taken place, the remedy provided by statute is not a civil action in the courts, nor even the exclusion of the evidence so obtained. Although in theory s 78 of PACE might be argued where such evidence is adduced (see page 14), s 9 of the Interception of Communications Act precludes examination or cross-examination in the course of any proceedings whatsoever which tends to suggest that an offence under s 1 has been committed. The exclusive remedy provided is to apply to the tribunal constituted under the Act for an investigation into the lawfulness of the suspected interception. The tribunal may quash the relevant warrant, order the destruction of copies of the intercepted material and order compensation to be paid to the applicant by the Secretary of State (s 7). In this respect, telephone tapping provides greater constitutional rights than other forms of electronic surveillance. A conversation that has been tape recorded as a consequence of unlawful interception will not necessarily be inadmissible in subsequent proceedings, but the fact of interception may entitle the aggrieved party to compensation.

It may be that car telephones are not covered by the above statutory provisions. This proposition has emerged from judicial comment made in a case which is believed to have involved the first prosecution in Britain for telephone bugging as a form of industrial espionage. The case was heard at Luton Crown Court in February 1988. Dixons (the electrical retail chain) authorised dossiers to be produced on the private lives of a few members of their senior staff. It was feared that senior staff may have been behind leaks of sensitive commercial data. The action was taken after Dixons failed in a major take-over bid. Two private detectives employed electronics experts to train microphones on the home of a former director of the company. A device was then used to pick up conversations by converting the vibrations of windows. The experts also connected a wire to the telephone line of the former director and intercepted his calls. The calls were recorded on a tape recorder hidden outside his home. Judge Rodwell stated that the training of microphones on the home of the ex-director of Dixons and the reception of conversations by such means could be regarded as "proper enquiries" but that the interception of the telephone line "overstepped the mark" (The Times 12 February 1988). A criminal offence had been committed under the Interception of Communications Act. In the course of his summing up, Judge Rodwell stated that the tapping of car telephones did not appear to be covered by statute. This is the only judicial interpretation to date on this issue. Concern already exists as to the extent of bugging of cellular radio networks. It may be that s 1 of the Interception of Communications Act (which refers to the interception of "a public telecommunication system") may need to be amended in the future. In any event, this case is of some significance in that it emphasises the distinction that exists between the taping of telephone conversations and the taping of other conversations or activities carried out by the subject under surveillance. The former is illegal unless carried out in accordance with statute. The latter is not illegal and is unlikely to provide the subject with any civil remedy.

4. The European Convention on Human Rights

Article 8 of the Convention has already been stated (see page 77). It formed the basis of Mr Malone's appeal to the European Court of Human Rights, and the case of *Malone* v *Metropolitan Police Commissioner* established that art 8 did not confer any right on a plaintiff in British courts to a declaration that an act of surveillance is in breach of the Convention. Article 8 therefore does not confer any direct protection against electronic surveillance. It protects through international pressure. If an activity is held (as in Mr Malone's case) to infringe the Convention, then legislation will follow to ensure that British law makes any future infringement illegal. However, art 8 does not prohibit interference with privacy by a public authority so far as this is necessary "for the prevention of disorder or crime" or for the "protection of the rights and freedom of others" (art 8(2), see page 77).

The issue of privacy and the scope of art 8 was discussed at international level by a conference of jurists. This conference, held in Stockholm in 1967, is referred to as *The Nordic Conference*. It concluded that the right to privacy should be recognised as a fundamental right of mankind. The Conference accepted that there had to be limitations to this right in a modern society and that the prevention of disorder or crime might justify measures taken in the sphere of criminal law:

(1) for the investigation of criminal offences and the detention of offenders;

(2) for the prosecution and punishment of offenders; and

(3) to prevent the commission of a criminal offence or the outbreak of a disorder which there are compelling grounds to believe is imminent.

It was recommended that the powers of the police should be defined in detail and that the offences in relation to which these powers could be used and the precise limits to their use should be laid down. No such statutory limits have been enacted in Britain, with the exception of the Interception of Communications Act.

The *Younger Committee Report on Privacy* (1972) drew a distinction between the civil and criminal law. The Committee recommended the creation of a new criminal offence of surreptitious surveillance by means of a technical device. To be guilty of the offence, the accused must intentionally interfere in a situation where the victim would be justified in believing that he had protected himself or his possessions from surveillance (whether by overhearing or by observation). It is to be noted that even if such a recommendation were ever to reach the statute book, it would probably not affect the rights of the police or others to record people taking part in activities in areas to which the public have access. The Committee rejected the concept of a general right to privacy creating a tortious action. Possible specific torts, that is a tort of unlawful surveillance and a tort of disclosure of information unlawfully acquired, were considered. The most favoured option was a development of the law on breach of confidence. It is, as stated earlier in this chapter, the one area of common law development towards a tort of invasion of privacy.

In 1981, the Law Commission considered the narrow issue of "breach of confidence" following the Younger Report and the decision of *Malone* v *Metropolitan Police Commissioner* concerning art 8 of the European Convention. The Commission (Report No. 110) stated "it is not our task in this report to consider the creation of criminal offences" (para 6.35). It was considered that:

> "the creation of a general right of privacy is beyond the scope of even an expanded law of breach of confidence. Liability in the case of a surveillance device must be based on the use or disclosure of information obtained by such a device." (para 6.36)

However, it was thought that a person should owe an obligation of confidence in respect of information acquired, *inter alia*, "by a device made or adapted solely for the purpose of surreptitious surveillance where the user could not without use of the device have obtained the information" (para 6.46). A caveat was provided that an obligation of confidence as above should not arise where the information has been obtained by a person in the course of the lawful exercise of an official function in regard to the security of the state or the prevention, investigation or prosecution of crime. The position of a private company using electronic surveillance for security purposes (such as a shop or bank) was not, apparently, considered by the Commission. However, it was considered that the obligation of confidence should not apply to information "in the public domain". Arguably all activities undertaken in public are matters of information in the public domain. Thus even had the recommendations of the Commission been implemented, no substantial change would have been made in the existing common law position concerning electronic surveillance of places to which the public have access, or to surveillance by the police. The right to privacy is therefore unlikely ever to exist in relation to those random public surveillance activities which cause the greatest outcry on the basis that personal liberties are being infringed. In fact the recommendations of the Commission have not yet been implemented. The tort of "breach of confidence" thus remains in an inchoate state and is, so far at least, an entirely common law concept.

Chapter 6

Tape recording police interviews

1. The current position

Ultimately, every police station in England and Wales will tape record interviews with suspects. At the time of writing, tape recording is taking place at those police stations equipped with sufficiently sound-proof rooms and the necessary machinery (for instance, five stations in the West Midlands police area are currently recording interviews). Section 60 Police and Criminal Evidence Act provides the statutory authority for this practice. Section 60(1)(a) states that it shall be the duty of the Secretary of State to issue a code of practice in connection with the tape-recording of interviews of persons "suspected of criminal offences which are held by police officers at police stations". Section 60(1)(b) provides that the Secretary of State is under the further duty:

> "to make an order requiring the tape recording of interviews of persons suspected of the commission of criminal offences, or of such descriptions of criminal offences as may be specified in the order, which are so held, in accordance with the code as it has effect for the time being".

The final draft of the Code of Practice was not laid before Parliament until July 1988. Thus the generalised use of tape recording is a relatively recent practice, despite its pioneering use, prior to the issue of the Code, in field trial areas and in a force-wide scheme in Essex. The fact that all police stations are not yet equipped to tape record interviews is a reflection of financial rather than legal limitations on the use of electronically recorded evidence.

2. The advantages and disadvantages of tape recording

The Home Office Research Report of 1988, based upon field trial experiments, concluded that the advantages of tape recording interviews far outweighed any disadvantages. This conclusion seems to be confirmed by the experience to date of those conducting the interviews. The main conclusions to be drawn from those working with taped interviews can be summarised as follows:

(a) It seems that a larger number of confessions are obtained in taped rather than untaped interviews. Further, the frequency with which information is given about other offences during interviews is also increased with taping.

(b) Proceedings are initiated against a higher proportion of suspects where interviews are tape recorded.

(c) The interviews are "free flowing" and are not hampered either because a police officer has to remember what he said or because there are gaps and pauses in the interviewing for a police officer to record the responses of the accused or the questions of another officer.

(d) There is some evidence (though it is by no means conclusive) that a higher proportion of defendants plead guilty to charges laid against them when the interview is taped.

(e) Although the Home Office Report concluded that there were some savings in police time writing up notes of interviews where taping took place, there is a real concern amongst police officers that an extra workload is placed upon the police in the time spent effecting a précis of the tape. The précis is of vital importance since, as will be explained later in this chapter, it will form the basis of the evidence tendered against the accused. It is at the discretion of a senior officer whether in a very serious case (such as murder) a full transcript should be used. The Code may be altered in the future to the extent that a précis will only be required in the case of a not guilty plea.

(f) There is some evidence to suggest that challenge to interview evidence is less likely when the interview is recorded. However, the police may be put in some difficulty when (due, essentially, to a resource problem) there may not be sufficient rooms available to interview suspects within the maximum period of detention permitted under PACE. This is particularly crucial in serious cases involving many defendants.

(g) It may be more difficult for a senior officer to control the interviews taking place where tapes replace written notes. He may have to listen to the whole tape of an interview to grasp the essence of the case.

Whatever the validity of the above conclusions, it is certain that tape recording is now a permanent feature of police interviews. The Code of Practice has therefore joined the other codes under PACE as part of the criminal process.

3. The Code of Practice

(a) General

Paragraph 1 of the *Code of Practice on Tape Recording* provides that the Code must be readily available for consultation by police officers, detained persons and members of the public at every police station where interviews with suspects are tape recorded. The code is in addition to the major *Code of Practice for the Detention, Treatment and Questioning of Persons by Police Officers* made pursuant to s 66 of PACE and does not detract in any way from those requirements. The "notes for guidance", which are printed at the conclusion of each paragraph, are not part of the formal provisions of the Code and are printed for the guidance of police officers and others (such as lawyers for the defence and members of the Crown Prosecution Service) applying the formal provisions.

(b) Recording and sealing of master tapes

Paragraph 2.1 provides that the tape recording of interviews shall be carried out openly "to instil confidence in its reliability as an impartial and accurate record of the interview". The notes for guidance provide that whilst, so far as possible, tape recording arrangements should be unobtrusive, it must be clear to the suspect that there is no opportunity to interfere with the tape recording equipment or the tapes. The Code provides, in para 2.2, that one tape (referred to throughout the code as the "master tape") will be sealed before it leaves the presence of the suspect. A second tape will be used as a working copy. The master tape is either one of two tapes used in a twin deck machine or the only tape used in a single deck machine. The working copy is either the second tape used in a twin deck machine or a copy of the master tape made by a single deck machine. As mentioned above, the master tape is sealed upon completion of the interview, before it leaves the presence of the suspect. The purpose of sealing the master tape is to establish confidence in the integrity of the tape. If it is necessary to make a working copy (when the interview is recorded upon a single deck machine) the copy must be made in the presence of the suspect and without the master tape having left his sight. Any further copies shall be made from the working copy, unless the working copy tape proves to be faulty. In that event the master tape may be copied, provided that this is done in the presence of the defence, police and Crown Prosecution Service and that the master tape is resealed thereafter (see para 6.2, page 98). The master tape will normally, therefore, remain sealed until trial, at which time it may become an exhibit in court (see para 5, page 98). Where a copy of the working copy is supplied to the defence after the interview has taken place, a charge of £5 is currently made.

(c) Interviews to be tape recorded

Paragraph 3.1 states that, subject to para 3.2, tape recordings shall be used at police stations to record any interview with a person who has been cautioned in respect of an indictable offence (including an either way offence). Thus offences which are summary only (such as many road traffic offences, taking a vehicle without authority and many criminal damage offences) come outside the ambit of the Code. The recording of interviews with those suspected of summary offences is not mandatory. There is difficulty, however, in that police may not be certain, at the stage of conducting the interview, what offence will in fact be charged. The only way to avoid this difficulty is to record all interviews with suspects, whatever the suspected crime may be. Paragraph 3.1 also makes mandatory the taping of interviews where, exceptionally, further questions are put to a suspect in respect of an indictable offence after he has been charged with or informed that he may be prosecuted for that offence. Further questions may only be put after charge when it is necessary to do so to prevent harm or loss to some other person or to the public, or "where it is necessary in the interests of justice that a person should have put to him and have an opportunity to comment on information that has come to light since he was charged" (para 17.5, Code C of the major Codes of Practice).

It is also mandatory to tape the responses of any person charged with an indictable offence (or informed that he may be prosecuted therefor), if that person is shown a written statement made by another person, or the content of an interview with another person. Where such statement or interview is shown, no reply or comment thereto shall be invited by the interviewing officer and the suspect must be cautioned (para 17.4 Code C of the major Codes of Practice). One method of bringing the content of an interview with another person to the notice of the suspect is, of course, to play him a tape recording of that interview.

Tape recording is not required in relation to interviews concerning offences of terrorism (with some exceptions), or in relation to interviews with a person suspected under the Official Secrets Act 1911 (para 3.2 of the Code). Terrorism is defined in accordance with the Prevention of Terrorism (Temporary Provisions) Act 1984 as "the use of violence for political ends and includes any use of violence for the purpose of putting the public or any section of the public in fear". The exclusion on recording interviews with suspected terrorists applies to offences connected with terrorism in Northern Ireland "or with terrorism of any other description other than terrorism connected solely with the affairs of the

United Kingdom or any part of the United Kingdom other than Northern Ireland" (para 3.2).

If it only becomes apparent during the course of an interview that the suspect may have committed a terrorist offence, the recording machine should be switched off as soon as terrorism is suspected. This exclusion gave rise to much criticism in July 1988 when the Code was laid before Parliament. Mr Douglas Hogg (Under-Secretary of State for the Home Office) defended the exclusion on the basis that "the sort of information that becomes available in the course of an interview following a terrorist offence can do much to damage national security" (Hansard 27 July 1988). It was emphasised that terrorism had been narrowly defined and that the primary purpose behind the offence would be looked at. Therefore (for instance), international drug smuggling would not be classed as a terrorist offence even though the crime might ultimately benefit a terrorist organisation.

By virtue of para 3.3, the custody officer may authorise the interviewing officer not to tape record the interview in certain instances. These are:

(i) that it is not reasonably practicable to tape the interview because of a failure of equipment or the non-availability of a suitable interview room or recorder and the authorising officer considers on reasonable grounds that the interview should not be delayed until the failure has been rectified or a suitable room or recorder becomes available. Where practicable, priority should be given to taping interviews with persons who are suspected of more serious offences; or

(ii) where it is clear from the outset that no prosecution will ensue.

In all cases the custody officer shall make a note in specific terms of the reasons for not tape recording. He should be prepared to justify his decision in each case, since a decision not to tape record an interview for any reason may be the subject of comment in court (see the notes for guidance to para 3.3).

The whole of each interview shall be tape recorded (para

3.5), including the taking and reading back of any statement. Where a person initially attends a police station on a voluntary basis, the interview must be recorded once the officer has grounds to believe that the person has become a suspect, that is, at the point at which he should be cautioned. It is to be noted that para 3 of the Code does not authorise the taping of interviews that should not be conducted due to the unfitness of the suspect through drink or drugs. Where a suspect is so unfit, he must not be questioned about an alleged offence except in very limited circumstances. Those circumstances are set out in Annex C to Code C of the major Codes of Practice. It states that a person "heavily under the influence of drink or drugs" may be interviewed in that state only if an officer of the rank of superintendent or above considers that delay will involve an immediate risk of harm to persons or serious loss or serious damage to property.

(d) The conduct of the interview

Paragraph 4.1 of the Code provides that when a suspect is brought into an interview room, the police officer shall, without delay, but in the sight of the suspect, load the tape recorder with previously unused tapes and set the machine to record. The tapes must be unwrapped or otherwise opened in the presence of the suspect. The notes for guidance provide that the police officer should attempt to estimate the likely length of the interview and ensure that the appropriate number of unused tapes and labels with which to seal the master tapes are available in the interview room. The officer "shall then tell the suspect formally about the tape recording" (para 4.2). He shall say:

(i) that the interview is being tape recorded;
(ii) his name and rank, and the name and rank of any other police officer present;
(iii) the name of the suspect and any other party present (for example, a solicitor);
(iv) the date, time of commencement and place of the interview; and
(v) that the suspect will be given notice about what will happen to the tapes.

The notes for guidance state that it will be helpful for the purpose of voice identification if the officer asks the suspect and any other persons present to identify themselves. The practical problems that face the police when tape recording interviews go further than voice identification, however. Ideally all interviews will eventually be video taped. In the meantime, specific interview techniques are needed to overcome difficulties raised by facial expression and gesture and "noises off". The ticking of a clock or the opening of a paper bag can sound quite alarming on tape. It will be necessary for the officer to use questions such as "why are you smiling?" or "why are you looking away?" Police officers are currently having to learn such techniques.

Before the interview commences, the police officer must caution the suspect. The normal form of caution should be used: "you do not have to say anything unless you wish to do so, but what you do say may be given in evidence". If it appears that a person does not understand what the caution means, the officer who has given it should explain it in his own words (notes for guidance). The officer should also make clear to the suspect that he has a right to silence, that is, that no adverse inference may be drawn from his refusal to answer questions. The right to silence is currently under review by the government.

There are special provisions relating to the deaf (para 4.4). If a suspect is deaf or there is doubt about his hearing ability, the police officer must take a contemporaneous note of the interview in accordance with the requirements of Code C of the major Codes of Practice under PACE as well as tape recording the interview. The purpose of this requirement is to give a deaf suspect equivalent rights of first hand access to the full interview record. However, the Royal National Institute for the Deaf is still concerned about the implications of this paragraph on deaf people (see Hansard 27 July 1988). The profoundly deaf generally use sign language, and there is concern that there should be a proper recording of what the deaf person has said or communicated. The Institute is therefore asking for the video taping of interviews with the deaf. The government considers that the use of a sign language interpreter is sufficient protection. The notes for guidance state that Code C of the Codes of Practice under PACE, relating to interpreters for the deaf or interviews with suspects who have difficulty understanding

English, continue to apply. Paragraph 14.4 of Code C of the main Codes of Practice provides that if a person is deaf (or there is doubt about his hearing ability) he must not be interviewed in the absence of an interpreter unless:

(i) he agrees in writing to be interviewed without one; or

(ii) an officer of the rank of superintendent or above considers that delay will involve an immediate risk of harm to persons or serious loss or serious damage to property.

Paragraph 14.7 states that where a person cannot communicate with a solicitor, because of language or hearing difficulties, an interpreter must be called. The interpreter may not be a police officer if the interpretation is needed for the purpose of obtaining legal advice. In other cases a police officer may interpret if the interview is tape recorded. There is no need, in the case of a tape recorded interview, to ensure that the interpreter makes a separate note of the interview.

There is a specified procedure to be adopted when tapes are changed during the course of an interview. Paragraph 4.8 provides that when the recorder indicates that the tapes have only a short time left to run, the police officer shall tell the suspect that the tapes are coming to an end and round off that part of the interview. If the police officer wishes to continue the interview, but does not already have a second set of tapes, he must obtain a set. The suspect may not be left unattended in the interview room. The new tapes must be opened in the presence of the suspect. Care must be taken to ensure that there is no confusion between the tapes. This may be done by marking the tapes with an identification number immediately after they are removed from the tape recorder.

Where a break is taken during the course of an interview and the interview room is to be vacated by the suspect, the fact that a break is to be taken, the reason for it and the time shall be recorded on tape (para 4.9). The tapes must then be removed from the tape recorder and the same procedures must be followed as at the conclusion of an interview (see page 95). Where the break is only a short one and both suspect and police officer are to remain in the interview room, the tapes need not be removed from the recorder. The fact that a break is to be taken, the reasons for it and the time, must still be recorded on the tape, and the time that the interview recommences must also be recorded on the tape. In this latter case, the recording will continue on the same tapes. Where there is a break in questioning, the interviewing officer must be sure that the suspect is aware that he remains under caution. If there is any doubt, the caution must be given again when the full interview resumes. The notes for guidance remind police officers that they may have to satisfy the court that a suspect understood that he was still under caution when the interview resumed. It is also suggested that the officer record on tape the reason for the break and that this is confirmed on tape by the suspect. This procedure will avoid arguments in court as to what may have occurred, for example as to whether the suspect was influenced to make admissions, during the break.

(e) Difficulties arising during the interview

One difficulty that might arise is that the suspect objects to the interview being tape recorded. This may occur either at the outset, during the course of the interview or during a break in the interview. Paragraph 4.5 states that, in this event, the police officer shall explain that the provisions of the Code require that the suspect's objections should be recorded on tape. When any objections have been recorded on tape or the suspect has refused to have his objections recorded, the officer may turn off the recorder. In this eventuality, he must state that he is turning off the recorder and give his reasons for so doing before he turns it off. The police officer must then make a written record of the interview in accordance with section 11 of Code C of the main Codes of Practice. (Section 11 provides for accurate and, where possible, contemporaneous notes to be made of all interviews held at police stations. If the written record is not made contemporaneously, the reasons why it is not so made must be recorded in the officer's notebook. The suspect should sign the written record. Any refusal by a suspect to sign notes of an interview must also be recorded). Paragraph 4.5 of the Code of Practice on Tape Recording states that if the officer reasonably considers that he may proceed to put questions to the suspect with the tape recorder still on, he may do so. However, the notes for guidance warn that a decision to continue recording against the wishes of the suspect may be the subject of comment in court. It is difficult to understand exactly what comment could then be made. The suspect does not, after all, have to say anything in answer to the recorded questions being put to him and he certainly has no choice in the matter whether the interview is commenced by way of tape recorded evidence. It is going to be extremely difficult for a suspect to challenge any admissions made to the police in a written record of the interview when he has refused to participate in a tape recorded interview.

A second difficulty may arise where a suspect indicates that he wishes to tell the police officer about other matters not directly connected with the offence of which he is suspected. The suspect may not wish these matters to be recorded on tape. In this event, para 4.7 provides that the suspect shall be given an opportunity to tell the officer about these matters after the conclusion of the formal interview. It will be interesting to see to what extent the courts will allow this "off the record" information to be used subsequently as evidence in court.

Where the suspect makes a complaint about his treatment during questioning, the fact that a complaint is made must be recorded and the custody officer must be informed (para 4.6). The notes of guidance provide that where the custody officer is called immediately to deal with the complaint, wherever possible the tape recorder should be left to run until the custody officer has entered the room and spoken to the person being interviewed. Continuation or determination of the interview is at the discretion of the interviewing officer pending action by an Inspector. If a complaint is made by or on behalf of a detained person about his treatment since arrest, a report must be made to an officer of the rank of inspector or above who is unconnected with the investigation. Where a complaint is made about a matter unconnected with observance of the Codes of Practice, the decision to continue the interview is at the discretion of the interviewing officer. Where the interviewing officer decides to continue with the interview, the suspect shall be told that the complaint will be brought to the attention of the custody officer at the conclusion of the interview. When the interview is concluded, the interviewing officer must, as soon as practicable, inform the custody officer of the existence and nature of the complaint made.

The final difficulty envisaged by the Code is a failure of the recording equipment. Paragraph 4.12 provides for various possibilities depending upon the nature of the breakdown. If all that is needed to remedy the breakdown is the insertion of new tapes, then the normal procedures for changing tapes should be adopted (see para 4.8, discussed at page 92). When the recording is resumed the officer must explain on tape what has happened and record the time that the interview recommences. If the failure is in the tape recorder rather than the tape, then a replacement machine may be found or the interview may be moved to another interview room where a machine is functioning correctly. In these situations also, the officer should explain on tape what has happened and record the time of the recommencement of the interview. If the failure is in the tape recorder and no replacement machine is readily available (perhaps because all the other interview rooms containing tape recorders are in use at the time) the interview may continue without being tape recorded. In that event, the custody officer must give authorisation for the interview to continue without delay (see para 3.3, page 89). If one of the tapes breaks during the interview, it must be sealed as a master tape in the presence of the suspect and the interview resumed where it left off. The unbroken tape should be copied and the original sealed as a master tape in the suspect's presence. If the tape breaks when a single deck machine is being used and the tape is one where a broken tape cannot be copied on available equipment, the tape should be sealed as a master tape in the suspect's presence and the interview begun again.

(f) At the conclusion of the interview

At the conclusion of the interview, the suspect must be offered the opportunity to clarify anything he has said and to add anything he may wish (para 4.14). Once the interview has terminated (and any written statement has been taken and read back to the suspect) the time shall be recorded and the tape recorder switched off (para 4.15). The master tape must be sealed with a "master tape label". This tape will then be treated as an exhibit of evidence in accordance with the Force Standing Orders. The police officer must sign the master tape label and ask the suspect and any third party (such as a solicitor) present to sign it also. If the suspect or third party refuses to sign the label, an officer of at least the rank of inspector (or, if one is not available, the custody officer) shall be called into the interview room and asked to sign it. Paragraph 4.16 states that the suspect must be handed a notice which explains the use which will be made of the tape recording and the arrangements for access to it.

(g) After the interview

After the interview, the police officer shall make a note in his notebook of the fact that the interview has taken place and has been recorded on tape. He must write down the time of the interview, its duration and date, and the identification number of the master tape (para. 5.1).

Paragraph 5.2 provides that where no proceedings follow in respect of the person whose interview was recorded, the tapes must nevertheless be kept securely. Paragraph 6 (see page 98) deals with tape security. It is to be noted that if no proceedings are taken, there is no fixed time for which the tapes must be held. This contrasts with the position where a suspect is charged with an offence. In the latter case, police practice in Essex (the only force-wide scheme operated prior to the drawing up of the final draft code) is to keep the tape for three years. If the suspect receives a sentence for a period of longer than three years, however, the tapes are kept for a period of ten years. This is to ensure that the tapes are still available in the event of an appeal and/or retrial.

Where proceedings do follow the interview, the officer must prepare a written record of the interview which will be signed by the officer. The interview record shall be exhibited to any written statement prepared by the officer. The notes for guidance provide that the officer may refresh his memory by listening to the working copy of the tape. The purpose of using the tape will be to act as a check on the accuracy of the interview record. As mentioned earlier in this chapter, one of the greatest police concerns is the time spent by officers effecting an interview record. This record is of great importance since it has four distinct purposes in subsequent proceedings. Firstly, it is used to enable the prosecutor to make an informed decision about the case on the basis of what was said at the interview. Secondly, it will be exhibited to the officer's witness statement and served on the defence under s 9 of the Criminal Justice Act 1967 or, in a case which goes for trial on indictment, under s 102 of the Magistrates' Courts Act 1980. In other words, it will form part of advance disclosure of witness statements to the defence. Its third function is to assist the prosecution to comply with the rules of advance disclosure. The Magistrates' Courts (Advance Information) Rules 1985 provide that in all cases where a case is triable either summarily or on indictment, the prosecution shall serve, at the request of the defence, either material parts of every written statement made by persons on whose evidence it is intended to rely in the proceedings, or a summary of such evidence. No mode of trial hearing can take place until the court is satisfied that the defendant is aware of his rights under the rules. As stated earlier (see page 87) it is only in the case of indictable (including either way) offences that tape recording of interviews is mandatory. Thus the Advance Information Rules will apply in most cases where the interview is tape recorded.

Fourthly, where the interview record is accepted by the defence, it will be used for the conduct of the case by the prosecution, the defence and the court. The notes for guidance therefore emphasise that the record shall comprise a balanced account of the interview including points in mitigation and/or defence made by the suspect. Where an admission is made, the question as well as the answer containing the admission shall be recorded *verbatim* in the record. Care should be taken to bring to the attention of the prosecutor, by means of a covering report, any material on the tape which might be regarded as prejudicial or inadmissible. The significance of acceptance of the interview record by the defence is explained in para 5.4 of the Code. Paragraph 5.4 provides that where the police officer's evidence of the interview (ie the interview record) is accepted by the defence, the evidence shall refer to the fact that the interview was tape recorded and may be presented to the court in the form of the interview record. Where the officer's evidence of the interview is not accepted by the defence, the police officer shall refer to the fact that the interview was tape recorded and shall produce the master tape as an exhibit. Thus if the interview record is accepted, it becomes evidence of the interview. If the interview record is not accepted, however, the tape itself becomes evidence of the interview. In this event, the notes for guidance provide that the production of the tape as an exhibit will have the effect of producing the content of the whole interview, subject to any decision on editing (for example, of inadmissible evidence) carried out on the direction of the Crown Prosecutor.

Thus the function of the master tape is to provide evidence as an exhibit in court, and the master tape should therefore not be unsealed before trial unless there are exceptional circumstances (see para 6, discussed below). Clearly it will save much time and expense if the interview record is accepted by the defence. The police must therefore endeavour to produce an accurate and balanced account of the interview as is possible. Where the interview record is not accepted, the officer shall inform the court of any transcription of the taped interview which has been made of which he is aware. This information must accompany the production of the master tape as an exhibit.

(h) Tape security

Paragraph 6 deals with the keeping and handling of tapes after the interview has taken place. Paragraph 6.1 provides that the officer in charge of each police station at which interviews with suspects are recorded shall make arrangements for master tapes to be kept securely, and their movements accounted for on the same basis as other material which may be used for evidential purposes, in accordance with Force Standing Orders. The seal on a master tape may not be broken by a police officer. Paragraph 6.2 states that if it is necessary to gain access to the master tape, the police officer shall arrange for its seal to be broken in the presence of a representative of the Crown Prosecution Service. The defendant or his legal adviser must be informed and given a reasonable opportunity to be present. If the defendant or his legal representative is present, he shall be invited to reseal and sign the master tape. If either refuses or neither is present, resealing shall be carried out by a representative of the Crown Prosecution Service. The master tape will be unsealed prior to trial only if the working copy proves faulty and it is therefore necessary to make a copy from the master tape. The notes for guidance emphasise that care should be taken of the working copies of tapes, since their loss or destruction will necessitate access to the master tape. Once committal proceedings have taken place and the master tape has been delivered to the Crown Court for their keeping, the Crown Prosecutor must apply to the chief clerk of the Crown Court Centre for release of the tape for unsealing (notes for guidance). As already mentioned on page 87, if the defendant asks to be shown a copy of the working copy of the tape, he must, at present, pay £5 for the facility. The consent of the Crown Prosecution Service will be necessary in case there is a disclosure of "sensitive material" (for example, privileged information). Paragraph 6.3 provides that where no criminal proceedings result, it is the responsibility of the chief officer of police to establish arrangements for the breaking of the seal on the master tape where this becomes necessary. It has already been pointed out (see (*g*) above) that there is no period prescribed during which tapes must be kept where no criminal proceedings result.

4. Tape recording of interviews by the defendant

It was acknowledged in the parliamentary debate on the Code, that solicitors "can use their own tape recorders when interviews take place". The Under-Secretary stated, however, that he would not encourage the practice (Hansard, 27 July 1988). If the defendant himself tapes a police interview, this can be admitted in evidence. In a case heard at Birmingham Crown Court on 24 November 1988, acquittals on charges of forgery and handling were returned at the direction of the judge. The defendant had smuggled tape recorders in his underpants to record interviews with the police in which he alleged he had been threatened that, if he did not confess, his children would be placed in care and his wife arrested. The quality of the recordings was enhanced by an expert and transcripts were provided to the court. Thus a tape recording of a police interview can come from a source other than the police themselves.

5. Breach of the Codes of Practice

The *Code of Practice on Tape Recording* is in addition to the other Codes of Practice which have been made pursuant to s 67 of PACE. Section 67 (11) states:

> "In all criminal and civil proceedings any such code shall be admissible in evidence; and if any provision of such a code appears to the court or tribunal conducting the proceedings to be relevant to any question arising in the proceedings it shall be taken into account in determining that question."

The most obvious question arising in criminal proceedings is the admissibility of any admission or confession made by the defendant where he alleges that one or more of the provisions of the Codes have been breached. Two sections of PACE afford the court the authority to exclude a confession. Section 76 provides that a confession can be challenged by the accused, or that the court may, of its own motion, raise the question of admissibility. The accused may represent to the court that the confession may have been obtained:

> "(a) by oppression of the person who made it; or
> (b) in consequence of anything said or done which was likely, in the circumstances existing at the time, to render unreliable any confession which might be made by him in consequence thereof." (s 76(2))

Once the issue is raised, the prosecution must prove beyond reasonable doubt that the confession was not so obtained. If it fails to do so, the confession must be excluded. Section 78 (which applies to all evidence including confessions) provides that the court has a discretion to exclude evidence on which the prosecution proposes to rely:

> "if it appears to the court that, having regard to all the circumstances, including the circumstances in which the evidence was obtained, the admission of the evidence would have such an adverse effect on the fairness of the

proceedings that the court ought not to admit it." (s 78(1)).

Section 78 is clearly wider than s 76, but it gives the court a *discretion* to exclude, whilst s 76 provides that the confession must be excluded if oppression or unreliability are not disproved by the prosecution. There have been many cases in the last year which have turned on the interpretation of these sections in relation to breaches of the Codes of Practice. It is not within the scope of this book to attempt a comprehensive analysis of the cases, but the following issues have arisen and may subsequently arise where the interview is tape recorded:

(i) Refusal of access to a solicitor after arrest (breach of s 58 PACE) does not mean that the confession will automatically be excluded. *R* v *Alladice* (1988) stated that no express sanction was contained in s 58 or elsewhere for such a breach. However, it was said that if the police had acted in bad faith in refusing access to a solicitor, the confession would be inadmissible under s 78 PACE. This approach has been affirmed in *R* v *Vernon* (1988). In that case a confession was excluded because the defendant was told that her solicitor could not see her since it was after midnight, and she was not told that a duty solicitor was arriving at the police station on behalf of another defendant. This can be contrasted with *R* v *Hughes* (1988) where, owing to a "mistake", the defendant was told that there was no duty solicitor available. It was held that the defendant had "genuinely consented to be interviewed" without a solicitor being present.

(ii) If the right to consult a solicitor has been restored, following a legitimate suspension of the right, the defendant must be specifically informed of this fact. In *R* v *Cochrane* (1988), the request to consult a solicitor was initially refused under s 58(8) PACE, on the basis that such consultation would hinder the recovery of property and the arrest of other suspects. The suspension of the right was then lifted. A statement in the custody record simply saying "incommunicado lifted" was insufficient. The defendant should have been asked what he wished to do about his reinstated right of access to a solicitor.

(iii) The courts have given a wide interpretation to the meaning of police "interview". The cases in this area are particularly important in relation to tape recorded interviews, since they deal with the possible problem of the police conducting "off the record" conversations with suspects before the formal taped interview. In *R* v *Foster* (1987), a brief interchange between the defendant and police, which was subsequently noted by police officers but not signed by the suspect, was excluded as being in breach of the Code. It was held that an exchange of remarks can be an "interview" if the subject matter of the conversation is relevant to the issue of whether an offence has been committed. Similarly in *R* v *Saunders (Rosemary)* (1988) an "off the record" interview was excluded, even though the defendant had stated that she would not be interviewed "with anything written down". The provisions of the Codes are mandatory and cannot be waived, even with the consent of the suspect. Preliminary questioning by the police will form part of the "interview" even if that questioning is conducted on the premises at which the accused is arrested (see *R* v *Malone and Docherty* (1988)) or in a police car before arrival at the police station. There is every possibility, therefore, that any admissions extracted by the police before the commencement of the tape recorded interview will be excluded under s 78 PACE.

(iv) A confession may be unreliable under s 76(2)(b) of PACE if the condition of the witness at the time that the confession is made is such that he is unfit to be interviewed; see *R* v *Trussler (Barry) and Another* (1988). The court will consider objectively the circumstances existing at the time of the confession. In *R* v *Everett* (1988) a man of forty-two with the mental age of eight years made admissions on tape to the police. The judge at first instance had ruled that the admissions should not be excluded. He had decided the matter simply by listening to the tapes of the interviews. He did not take into account the

> medical evidence of the mental condition of the appellant. On appeal, it was held that the admissions should have been excluded. It was not material what the police officers thought of the appellant's mental condition. What was material was the objective medical evidence as to the suspect's mental condition. Where any query arises therefore as to the physical or mental fitness of the suspect, no interview should be conducted without specialist advice as to the fitness or capacity of the suspect to be interviewed. This is so even where the interview is thereby delayed until the suspect is no longer drunk or under the influence of drugs or until an appropriate adult is found to be present during the interview of a mentally handicapped suspect.

It has to be stated, however, that challenges to the admissibility of confessions and challenges to the content of police interviews in particular, will be reduced when the tape recording of interviews becomes universal practice. Both defendant and police will benefit. The defendant is better protected against undue pressure and misrepresentation by the police, and the police will face fewer allegations that interviews have been conducted improperly.

Appendix

Home Office Circular 76/1988 dated 17 August 1988 The Police and Criminal Evidence Act 1984

Section 60: The Tape Recording of Police Interviews with Suspects at Police Stations

THE OBJECTIVES OF TAPE RECORDING

3. The purpose of the tape recording procedures is to provide an accurate and reliable account of police interviews with suspects in police stations. This will provide an effective safeguard for the rights of suspects. It should also reduce challenge to the admissibility of prosecution evidence based on these interviews. In addition, tape recording offers scope for savings in police time. The length of interviews may be expected to decline as interview techniques improve and the need to make handwritten contemporaneous notes is removed. The overall time taken for the process of interviewing and recording will thereby be reduced. In many cases it will also become possible for interviews which are tape recorded to be conducted by one police officer only. Chief officers will wish to identify and monitor these and other effects of tape recording. HM Inspectors of Constabulary will be asked to discuss them with chief constables in their annual force inspections.

THE CODE OF PRACTICE

Background to the Code

4. The procedures set out in the Code are based on those adopted in field trials—carried out in five force areas over a period of two years—and amended after further consultations. The Code has been discussed by the National Steering Committee on the field trials on which all interested agencies within the criminal justice system, including the police service, were represented.

Scope of the Code of Practice

5. The Code of Practice on tape recording deals with police procedures. As with the other Codes of Practice issued under the

Police and Criminal Evidence Act 1984, a breach of its provisions by a police officer will constitute a disciplinary offence. Consequently, the Code can regulate only the conduct of police officers and those aspects of their conduct which can be subjected to disciplinary control. A court may exclude as inadmissible evidence obtained in breach of its provisions. The tape recording of interviews with suspects, therefore, will have important implications not only for the police but also for other participants in the criminal justice system. It is the purpose of this Circular to supplement the Code by providing guidance on matters which fall outside the scope of the Code. Tape recording of interviews with suspects has had already, and will continue to have, important implications for and effects on all participants in the criminal justice system. In addition to laying down procedures for the police this Circular also identifies best practice in areas which affect other agencies in the criminal justice system. The Secretary of State hopes, therefore, that those who are concerned with the implementation of the new arrangements will have regard to its provisions.

IMPLEMENTATION OF TAPE RECORDING

6. Section 60(1)(b) of the Police and Criminal Evidence Act 1984 places on the Secretary of State a duty to make an order requiring the tape recording of interviews held in accordance with the Code of Practice issued under section 60(1)(a). It is his intention to make such orders in relation to individual police force areas or parts thereof after each force has made satisfactory arrangements for the tape recording of interviews. Orders will be made following consultation with the chief officer of police concerned. Before any order is made it is open to any chief officer, in consultation with the local chief crown prosecutor to make informal arrangements for tape recording and to put them into effect on a trial basis. In doing this, it would be advisable for chief officers to have regard to the provisions of the Code of Practice. This will allow their officers to familiarise themselves with its procedures and requirements and will remove the risk of misconceived challenge in court. When he is satisfied that the informal arrangements are working properly and can be put on a mandatory basis, the chief officer should approach the Home Office so that the Home Secretary can be invited to make the necessary Order.

7. It is the Government's intention that the tape recording of interviews with suspects should become standard police practice throughout England and Wales by 1991. A phased introduction will spread the costs and give time for all concerned in the criminal justice system to adapt to the new procedures and resolve any

difficulties which arise. The rate at which individual forces proceed within the period is a matter for the judgement of each chief officer in consultation with other agencies in the criminal justice system and having regard to the availability of resources. It will be important for the establishment of satisfactory tape recording arrangements for chief officers to take account of their implications in particular for the courts, prosecution and defence. They should agree locally with the chief crown prosecutor the timescale for the introduction of tape recording in the force area and how the programme of implementation should be phased. These matters should be considered at an early stage to ensure that plans are based on a firm assessment of their implications for all concerned.

Steering Committees

8. The National Steering Committee will continue in existence to keep arrangements for tape recording in England and Wales under review. Police forces which participated in the field trials found it helpful to establish local steering committees. These helped to foster mutual understanding between the different agencies in the criminal justice system by providing a means through which information could be shared and problems resolved. It is recommended that chief officers should establish steering committees in their force area to plan, oversee and help to monitor the introduction of tape recording arrangements and their implementation. The chief officer will wish to consult the presiding judge of the local circuit through the circuit administrator to invite him to nominate a chairman for the steering committee and to invite the Crown Prosecution Service, Police Authority, magistracy, justices' clerks, local law societies, local Bar (if there is one), the Regional Legal Aid Director, HM Customs and Excise [contact, in writing, HM Customs and Excise Investigation Division, Harmsworth House, Bouverie Street, London EC4Y 8BS], other police forces (if appropriate) and police staff associations to be represented on it. The terms of reference for the field trials local steering committees may serve as a model for the area committees: "to co-ordinate locally the introduction and operation of tape recording and provide a forum for the review and resolution of issues encountered or anticipated locally, including access to tapes by the defence, arrangements for playing tapes in court and the presentation of tapes in evidence".

9. Where other authorities with responsibility for investigating offences and conducting prosecutions are planning to tape record interviews with suspects they must, under section 67(9) of the Police and Criminal Evidence Act, have regard to the relevant

provisions of the Code of Practice. They will need to be kept informed of the progress of tape recording in each force area and of agreements reached in local steering committees bearing on prosecuting and court practice. Chief officers will wish to consider, or invite their local steering committee to consider, how this might best be achieved for other authorities normally conducting prosecutions in their area. (If necessary the Home Office, F2 Division, can advise on the appropriate contact points for the prosecuting authorities concerned.)

10. Chief officers and local steering committees will also wish to keep in mind the interest of coroners. Tapes of police interviews are sometimes needed for inquests. It will be helpful for coroners to know where forces are tape recording and about any relevant agreements reached in steering committees concerning court practice.

TRAINING, EQUIPMENT AND INTERVIEW ROOMS

Training

11. Conducting an interview which is tape recorded will be a new experience for police officers who will require careful training. They will need to be aware of the contribution which they can make to the successful recording of the interview through preparation before it is conducted and the observance of simple techniques to avoid unintelligible conversation during the course of the interview. Training will also have an important role to play in helping police officers to prepare satisfactory written records of tape recorded interviews. It will be important to ensure that the training is approached in a positive manner, emphasising the advantages to the police and seeking to arouse interest in it as a welcome advance in procedures. The training itself should give officers receiving it an opportunity to gain "hands on" experience with the equipment, to familiarise themselves with it and to practise the skill of conducting interviews and preparing written records of interviews. It should help them to recognise non-verbal communication during interviews and the need to guard against causing extraneous noises (eg rustling papers) or talking over the suspect's voice. It is also likely to be helpful to provide familiarisation opportunities at the police station level for local lawyers, magistrates and clerks to ensure they have an opportunity to see the arrangements made by the police and to understand the tape recording procedures. A training video about the written record of interview has been prepared and is available to all forces.

Equipment

12. It is a matter for each chief officer to decide what equipment is best suited to the needs of his force. Some equipment, which was used in the field trials, has been tested by the Home Office Scientific Research and Development Branch who are prepared to offer advice on it [Available on application to the Information Desk, Home Office Scientific Research and Development Branch, Woodcock Hill, Sandridge, Herts, AL4 9HQ]. Other equipment is also available and chief officers will wish to consider its suitability. They may find it helpful to bear the following points in mind when reaching a decision. The Code of Practice requires that the master tape shall be unwrapped, placed in the tape recorder and, after use, sealed again, in the suspect's presence. This is intended to provide a simple and visible method of reassuring the suspect that the tape cannot be tampered with. The requirements of the Code may be met by either a twin deck or a single deck tape recorder. It will, however, be necessary to make a working copy of the master tape before the latter is sealed. In the case of a twin deck machine this will be the second tape in the machine and will be made simultaneously with the master tape. In the case of a single deck machine, the working copy must be made after the conclusion of the interview and care must be taken to ensure that the master tape does not leave the suspect's presence while it is being copied.

13. Chief officers will also wish to take account of other practical considerations such as reliability of the equipment, the simplicity of its controls (to reduce the risk of mistakes by inexperienced officers), the manufacturers' arrangements for service and repair and the compatibility of tapes with other equipment in use by other police forces and by other agencies in the criminal justice system. Chief officers will also wish to take account of additional equipment, other than the tape recorder, which will be necessary to copy and to play back tapes in police stations. They will also wish to bear in mind the desirability of its compatibility with existing equipment in typing pools and court rooms as well as in lawyers' offices. Any of the generally available equipment is likely to prove satisfactory provided it is durable and easy to use.

Interview Rooms

14. Chief officers will wish to consider the location and number of interview rooms which their forces will require for tape recording. There is no requirement to locate all interview rooms in or near cell blocks or in secure areas of police stations. This would be expensive and would be unnecessary for interviews with suspects where no security is required, or where security is undesirable. It

will normally be preferable to seek to adapt existing interview rooms wherever they are located and to ensure that a reasonable proportion of them are outside the cell block areas. The numbers of rooms equipped for tape recording will depend on the likely demand. Advice on this is provided in Annex B of this Circular. It will be important to ensure that the minimum necessary provision is made to avoid unnecessary expenditure. Short periods spent waiting for a heavily used room to become available will be preferable to the under-use of interview rooms. Forces should be careful not to aim to provide sufficient rooms to meet peak demands.

15. When considering what building and equipment arrangements are necessary to facilitate tape recording, chief officers will wish to bear in mind the objective of providing the minimum level of sound proofing that is consistent with an intelligible, recognisable record of the interview. It is not necessary to eliminate all background noise or reduce it to a totally inaudible level. Such noise can be tolerated provided it is still possible to hear clearly the interview and recognise the voices of the participants. This is an important consideration in deciding the amount of building work which is necessary to improve the acoustics of interview rooms. Given the potential expense involved in soundproofing, it is desirable to keep this to a minimum. Guidance on the acoustic treatment of interview rooms and estimating costs has been provided by SRDB in "Acoustic Treatment of Rooms—A Step by Step Guide" which has been distributed to police forces. Further copies are available on request (from the Information Desk, Home Office Scientific Research and Development Branch, Woodcock Hill, Sandridge, Herts, AL4 9HQ).

THE INTERVIEW

Interviews to be taped

16. The Code requires that all interviews with persons suspected of offences which are triable on indictment (including offences triable either way) must be tape recorded. Although there is nothing in the Code to prevent a chief officer deciding he wishes his force to tape record interviews in any type of summary offences once his force has established satisfactory arrangements for tape recording in indictable offences (including offences triable either way), chief officers are advised not to move to the general tape recording of interviews in summary cases for the present. Any extension to summary cases should be limited, for the time being, to those with special features which make it desirable for an interview to be tape recorded. If there is any doubt at the time of interview about

whether or not the offence will be a summary offence or an either way offence, the interview should be tape recorded. Before any future move to the general tape recording of interviews in summary cases takes place, chief officers should agree on the arrangements with the local chief crown prosecutor and seek the views of their area steering committees.

Interviews with suspects who are deaf and/or dumb

17. Although the value of a taped record of an interview is diminished with a suspect whose ability to hear or speak is seriously impaired, it is still significant as a record of the manner in which the interview was conducted by the interviewing officer and failure to provide a taped record might provide grounds for challenge by the defence. Paragraphs 4.63 N and 4.63 O of the consolidated circular to the police draw attention to the need to be alert to the difficulties of communicating with deaf people (especially those who may be prelingually deaf) and the importance of taking care to ensure that there is no doubt about the need for an interpreter. Paragraph 14.4 of Code C, which requires that interpreters must be provided unless the suspect expressly waives this right, applies. In practice, interpreters are likely to be required for all taped interviews unless it is apparent that the suspect is skilled in lip reading and can express himself clearly, or the exceptional circumstances envisaged in Annex C to Code C apply. In any event, even if the suspect is willing (or prefers) to proceed without an interpreter, it is at the interviewing officer's discretion to decide that one should nonetheless be present in the interests of making a clear recording. The requirement in paragraph 4.4 of the Code of Practice on Tape Recording—that contemporaneous notes should be taken of all interviews with people who are deaf or whose ability to hear is in doubt—is intended to give them equivalent rights of first hand access to the full interview record as other suspects. It might be advisable for the interpreter to take notes in case he is required to give evidence in court. Deaf suspects may articulate words the meaning of which is modified by sign language undetectable on tape and this may lead to questions about the interpreter's version of what the suspect intended to say. If the interpreter cannot easily take notes because he or she is communicating with the suspect in sign language, it would be sensible for the police officer to write down the questions and answers on his or her instruction and for the interpreter to certify the accuracy of the record.

Interviews with terrorist suspects and persons suspected of an offence under section 1 of the Official Secrets Act 1911

18. Paragraph 3.2(a) of the Code of Practice provides that the Code does not apply to interviews with persons arrested under section 12(1)(a) of the Prevention of Terrorism (Temporary Provisions) Act 1984. Section 12(1)(a) permits the arrest without warrant of a person reasonably suspected to be guilty of an offence under section 1 (offences connected with a proscribed organisation), section 9 (offences connected with breach of an exclusion order) or section 10 (contribution towards acts of terrorism) of the Act. An exemption from the Code is not needed for interviews with people arrested under other provisions of the Act in respect of whom there is no, or is not yet any, suspicion of the commission of a criminal offence. This is because the Code only applies to interviews with persons suspected of the commission of criminal offences and after caution. Paragraph 3.2(a) of the Code similarly exempts interviews with persons being questioned in respect of an offence which it is believed on reasonable grounds is connected to terrorism as defined in section 14(1) of the Act or committed in furtherance of the objectives of an organisation engaged in such terrorism. Section 14(1) defines terrorism as "the use of violence for political ends [including] any use of violence for the purpose of putting the public or any section of the public, in fear."

19. Paragraph 3.2(a) of the Code applies only to those suspected of offences connected with terrorism of the kind described in section 12(3) of the Prevention of Terrorism (Temporary Provisions) Act (broadly, international terrorism and Northern Irish terrorism). Interviews with people suspected of other acts of terrorism (that is, broadly, non-Northern Irish domestic terrorism) should be tape recorded in compliance with the other provisions of the Code.

20. Paragraph 3.2(b) of the Code exempts interviews with those suspected on reasonable grounds of an offence under section 1 of the Official Secrets Act 1911.

21. Interviews with terrorist suspects and persons suspected of an offence under section 1 of the Official Secrets Act 1911 were not included in the tape recording field trials and there is no intention that they should be generally recorded. In the majority of cases it will be obvious whether an interview relates to terrorism and falls outside the Code. If however there is any significant doubt, the decision not to tape the interview should be referred to an officer of not lower than Superintendent rank. If it only becomes clear during the course of an interview which is being tape recorded that the interviewee may have committed an offence to which

paragraph 3.2 applies, the interviewing officer should turn off the tape recorder, having first recorded that he is doing so. He should then consult an officer of at least Superintendent rank for authority to continue the interview without the use of tape recording unless he believes on reasonable grounds that to interrupt the interview would seriously hinder the investigation. In that case he should continue the interview without the use of tape recording, but he should report his actions to an officer of not lower than Superintendent rank as soon as practicable after the conclusion of the interview.

Sealing the Tape

22. The Code of Practice requires that when an interview comes to an end the cassette(s) of the master tape(s) should be sealed and signed by the suspect. If the suspect declines to do this the seal should be signed by the appropriate officer (see section 4.15 of the Code). At Annex C to this Circular is a specimen form for this purpose which chief officers may find helpful.

TAPES IN EVIDENCE

The Record of a Tape Recorded Interview

23. The successful introduction of tape recording depends on the provision by the police of an adequate written record of the contents of an interview which is acceptable to the crown prosecutor and the defence—so as to keep to a minimum the need for the tape to be listened to or for a full transcript to be provided. Under the Prosecution of Offences Act 1985 it is the statutory duty of the Crown Prosecution Service to take over the conduct of all criminal proceedings (other than specified proceedings) instituted on behalf of the police. The Crown Prosecution Service must be in a position to consider whether there is sufficient evidence to justify a prosecution and, if so, whether the prosecution is in the public interest. While the length of the record of an interview will vary as a reflection of the nature of the interview and the case, it must always provide an accurate and reliable account of the relevant parts of the interview upon which the Crown Prosecution Service can rely. It is inevitable that if the standard of records of interview deteriorates the crown prosecutor will return them to be re-submitted in adequate form.

24. Records of tape recorded interviews serve a four-fold purpose: first, to enable the prosecutor to make informed decisions about the case on the basis of what was said in the interview; secondly, to be exhibited to the officer's witness statement and used pursuant to section 9 of the Criminal Justice Act 1967 or section 102 of the

Magistrates' Courts Act 1980; thirdly, to enable the prosecutor to comply with the rules of advance disclosure; and fourthly, where the record is accepted by the defence, to be used for the conduct of the case by the prosecution, the defence, and the court.

25. Police officers who prepare interview records must therefore always be aware of their purpose and of the need for them to serve as an accurate and reliable basis on which others in the criminal justice system can make informed decisions. Experience in the field trials demonstrated that where summaries were properly prepared they proved satisfactory for the requirements of the prosecution, defence and courts and the expense of listening to tapes or transcribing them could normally be avoided. A draft force order about the preparation and submission of evidence to the Crown Prosecution Service is attached at Annex D of this Circular. Special emphasis on training will need to be given to the preparation of the record of interview; the subject is covered in a training video (see paragraph 11).

26. The record of interview will reflect what the interviewing officer is likely to say if required to give evidence. Where the tape recorded interview contains material believed to be "sensitive" as defined by the Attorney General's Guidelines for the disclosure of unused material to the defence, or where it contains prejudicial or inadmissible material, the officer should draw such matters to the attention of the prosecutor by means of a covering report.

Listening to the Tape

27. When the prosecutor receives the case papers he will generally expect to rely on the record of the interview thereby keeping to a minimum the occasion on which the Crown Prosecution Service have to listen to a tape or read a transcript.

28. It should not be assumed that defence solicitors will feel the need to take advantage of the right of access to copies of tape recordings in all cases, or that when they do so they will feel the need to listen to the tape in its entirety. In this context the Standing Committee on Criminal Law of the Law Society has approved the following guidance:

> "Whether or not a solicitor listens to a tape recording of a police interview with a client is a matter which falls to be considered within the solicitor's general duty of care in advising a client. The discharge of that duty of care in relation to tape recorded interviews will depend *inter alia* on the instructions received by the solicitor about the events covered by the tape recording. There can, therefore, be no requirements for a solicitor to listen to such a tape recording in every case."

Transcriptions of Tapes

29. The tape recording arrangements can succeed only if full transcribing of tape recorded interviews is kept to an irreducible minimum. Experience in the field trials indicated that except in complex cases such transcripts are rarely necessary. The decision as to whether a transcript of an interview will be needed must be based on the circumstances of each individual case, having regard to its complexity, the difficulty of summarising the interview evidence, of adequately pursuing the investigation, or of adequately reviewing a case or conducting a prosecution without a transcript. Altough these factors may be present in any type of crime they are more likely to arise in the more serious offences, such as murder, fraud, large scale robberies, or multiple rapes.

30. In complex cases where a transcription of all or a substantial part of a taped interview proves necessary for use by the police in the investigation, the police will provide a copy of it to the Crown Prosecution Service who will be responsible for its disclosure to the defence. There may be circumstances where, although a transcript has not proved necessary for the purposes of the investigation, it may be the only practical way for the police to present the evidence to the Crown Prosecution Service having regard to the seriousness or complexity of the case. If such occasions do arise, it is recommended that the arrangements for the preparation of this transcription should be discussed and agreed locally at an appropriately senior level in both services.

31. If the defence wish to transcribe a tape or part of a tape which is in the possession of the police, the police should provide them with a copy of the tape so that they can make their own arrangements for the transcription to be made. There is no requirement on the police to undertake the transcription but if they are willing to do this it would be proper to make an economic charge for the costs they incur.

32. Since the provisions of a transcript can be very expensive, the cost may be disallowed on taxation. Arrangements have therefore been made for prior consideration by the relevant authorities of applications for transcripts. If a transcript is prepared with prior approval the party concerned will not run the risk of having the expense disallowed. The arrangements for prior consideration are as follows:

(a) *Legally-aided defence:* the solicitor should apply to the Legal Aid Committee;

(b) *Non-legally-aided defence:* for cases to be heard on indictment, it is open to the non-legally-aided defence to apply to the Court for an indication of the reasonableness of the costs likely to be incurred. In indictable cases to be heard summarily, application may be made similarly to the justices' clerk.

33. All applications should be made in the first instance in writing and, for cases to be heard on indictment under (b) above, should be made through the chief clerk.

34. These arrangements will enable the defence to make an application, in effect, *ex-parte* so that there is no danger of the nature of the defence being revealed to the prosecution. It is, however, desirable that the possibility of both parties making a transcript unknown to each other should be guarded against. Where a prosecution takes place, the prosecution will provide the defence with a copy of any transcript which it has in its possession. Similarly, where a transcript is obtained by the defence, a copy will be made available to the prosecution unless the proper conduct of the defence precludes it.

35. The party making the transcript may wish to inform the other party of the fact so that the risk of the other party applying for adjournments to check the accuracy of the transcript may be reduced. Where a transcript is in the possession of the defence and the prosecution, any change to it may be made by one party only with the consent of the other. Where there remains doubt about the accuracy of the transcript which cannot be resolved before the case comes to trial, the normal rules as to the burden of proof will apply, and the matter will normally be resolved by playing the tape in court.

Disclosure of Tape Recorded Interviews to the Defence

36. After a suspect has been interviewed he should be given a copy of the notice at Annex E explaining the tape recording arrangements and how he may obtain a copy if he is prosecuted. The case will be referred to the Crown Prosecution Service in the usual way and all questions relating to the disclosure of evidence, including tapes, or of editing sensitive or inadmissible material, are matters which will be carried out under the direction of the crown prosecutor. Editing any tape without error can be difficult. Regional Police Technical Support Units have some limited specialised facilities for editing and may be able to advise in cases of doubt.

37. The Crown Prosecution Service will be guided by the same rules on disclosure that apply to any other form of evidential material. These are based on the principle that the defendant or the legal representative will of right have access to material, including tape recordings, which may be material as evidence.

38. It is in the spirit of the tape recording arrangements that the content of the record of the taped interview should be agreed between the prosecution and the defence before the case comes to court. With that in mind the Secretary of State commends to chief officers the practice of serving with any copy of the tape sent to the defence a form similar to that reproduced at Annex F. In the event of a minor challenge to the accuracy of the record of interview being made by the defence or complaint made about the omission of any point, this should be brought to the attention of the crown prosecutor who will return it to the police for the officer to consider and (with Crown Prosecution Service guidance as appropriate) to prepare a revised record of interview. Where the prosecution and the defence are unable to agree on a record of interview it will normally be appropriate to play the tape or relevant part(s) thereof in court. If the defence give notice that they will require an officer to appear at trial to prove the tape in accordance with the guidelines laid down by the Court of Appeal in *R* v *Rampling* [The Times, 29 August 1987] this should be brought to the attention of the crown prosecutor.

39. Copies of tapes should not be supplied to the Crown Prosecution Service unless they so request. Local arrangements should be agreed for providing access to tapes by the defence. Since tapes are held by the police, the defendant or his legal representative may be offered access to them either by being provided with copies or by listening to them at a police station.

40. Unadmitted employees of defence solicitors should normally be given the same right of access but should have the prior authority of an admitted solicitor. In the case of unrepresented defendants remanded in custody who seek access to tapes, copies will either be sent to them through the Prison Governor or placed with the prisoner's property at his second or subsequent remand hearing. Alternatively, where it has been agreed with the prison authorities that prisoners are normally delivered into the custody of the police for escort to court, arrangements may be made for an unrepresented prisoner to listen to the tape at the police station before his remand hearing. This is not intended to suggest that the prison should arrange an escort specially for that purpose.

41. The police may, on request, permit the defence to listen to the tape recording of an interview before charge unless, in their view, there are good reasons for believing that to comply with such a request would impede the course of justice. However, if a suspect is about to be charged and there is no intention to interview him further, it will normally be appropriate to charge the suspect and refer the request to the Crown Prosecution Service for disclosure in the normal way.

Court Play-Back Arrangements

42. Equipment for the playing back of tapes in magistrates' and crown courts will be provided by the courts themselves.

43. It should not be necessary in court proceedings to provide a standard of reproduction of tapes higher than that normally achieved for the live human voice. The Home Office Scientific Research and Development Branch can provide on request information about types of playback equipment which are simple to set up and can reproduce intelligible tapes of police interviews with suspects at low cost, in the acoustic conditions to be found in most courts. Equipment costing between £250 and £400 per set, including any necessary speakers, has been tried. Whatever quality of playback equipment is provided, a poorly taped recording is unlikely to be heard clearly in court. The Scientific Research and Development Branch have provided guidance (see paragraph 15) to help ensure that interview rooms are protected against levels of outside noise which are likely to seriously impair the intelligibility of the recording and about recording equipment which was found to be generally satisfactory during the field trials in rooms acoustically treated as recommended. In addition, chief officers will wish to ensure that interviewing officers are aware of the need to seek to minimise interference to the recording from, for example, talking over the suspect's voice or from extraneous noise such as rustling papers.

44. Regional Technical Support Units should be able to advise about repair and enhancement of damaged or poor tape recordings and how these might be played in court if necessary. It will be for the crown prosecutor to decide whether and what part of an unsatisfactory tape should be referred to the Regional Technical Support Unit for their assistance. He will also make the arrangements for the defence to hear any enhanced tape and compare it with the original. The Units may also be able to advise about essential editing which the crown prosecutor directs should be done (see paragraph 36). If a tape is referred to a Regional Technical Support Unit it should be the second tape (not the master tape) on a twin-deck machine and a copy tape if a single-deck machine has been used. The procedures described in part 6 of the Code of Practice for unsealing master tapes should then be followed except that the unsealed master-tape should be placed in a bag with a seal signed by the defendant or his legal adviser, or by the representative of the Crown Prosecution Service if they refuse or are not present. The tape in its sealed bag should then be delivered by hand where possible, or by recorded or registered post, to the Regional Technical Support Unit who will return it to the crown prosecutor. If tapes are sent by recorded or registered

post, it is advisable that they should be accompanied by a list identifying the tape(s) and a note explaining which part(s) need attention and why.

Taped Interviews with Officers who are the Subject of a Complaint

45. There is no requirement in the Code of Practice to tape record an interview with a police officer against whom a complaint has been made of behaviour which does not amount to an allegation of a criminal offence: but if the interview is tape recorded a copy of the tape(s) should be included in the papers sent to the Police Complaints Authority with the memorandum submitted under section 90(5) of the Police and Criminal Evidence Act 1984. If the interview takes place in the course of an investigation carried out under the supervision of the Authority, a copy of the tape(s) should accompany the investigating officer's report submitted to the Authority under section 89(6).

Retention of tapes

46. Master tapes should not be stored for any longer than other forms of evidential material after a case (including any appeal) has been finally closed. Working and other copies need to be retained only until the case has been finally closed. Chief officers may wish to agree storage time with their local chief crown prosecutor, taking into account local circumstances, but in general need not store tapes for any longer than paper records.

The Disposal of Tapes

47. It is for chief officers to decide how tapes in their keeping should be disposed of when the period for retention has passed. Where satisfactory arrangements can be made to wipe the tapes clean so that there is no risk of breach of confidence in so doing, the cleaned tapes might be offered for sale or might be used for other purposes. It should be noted that section 4.1 of the Code of Practice requires that only unused tapes should be used as master tapes and working copies in the tape recording of interviews with suspects. Old tapes which have been wiped clean may however be used to make additional copies where this is necessary.

* * * * *

ANNEX D: DRAFT FORCE ORDER

PRESENTATION AND SUBMISSION OF EVIDENCE TO CROWN PROSECUTION SERVICE

Tape Recorded Interviews: Police Officers' Statements—Record of Tape Recorded Interview

As a general rule, where an officer conducts a tape recorded interview with a suspected person, the officer shall prepare a Record of Tape Recorded Interview. This will not be necessary where the interview produces no evidence and there is no other evidence on which a prosecution can be considered or if for another reason no case file is to be submitted.

Records of Taped Interviews have a four-fold purpose: firstly, to enable the prosecutor to make informed decisions on the case on the basis of what was said in the interview; secondly, to be exhibited to the officer's witness statement and used pursuant to Section 9 of the Criminal Justice Act 1967 or Section 102 of the Magistrates' Courts Act 1980; thirdly, to enable the prosecutor to comply with the rules of advance disclosure; and, fourthly, where the Record of Taped Interview is accepted by the defence, to be used for the conduct of the case by the prosecution, the defence and the court.

The Record of Taped Interview must provide an accurate and reliable account of the relevant parts of the interview upon which the crown prosecutor will rely in any subsequent prosecution. This should include where appropriate evidence to establish intent, other ingredients of the offence and possible lines of defence. It must also be fair and balanced and reflect any matters to the benefit of the accused including mitigation (such as expressions of remorse or a desire to co-operate or assist in the recovery of property, etc).

Officers are reminded that the tape recording of an interview does not preclude a suspect electing to make a written statement under caution. Such statements should be taken whilst the tape is running. When this occurs the Record of Taped Interview may be shorter if in the officer's opinion the written statement under caution accurately summarises what the suspect said during the interview.

The Record of Taped Interview may generally be written in the third person; however, salient points must be recorded verbatim. These will include:

(a) any questioning of or statements by the suspect on intent, dishonesty, self-defence, consent, the granting of bail or discussions concerning alternative pleas or charges; and
(b) admissions by the suspect to the offence(s) under investigation and any other criminal offences for which he may be prosecuted.

It will be necessary to record verbatim both the question(s) and the answer(s) containing the admissions. Statements such as "the accused admitted the offence" should never appear in a Record of Taped Interview. Furthermore, where the suspect provides an equivocal response to a question going to the heart of the issue, eg. "I can't remember taking the packet of peas, but as you found it on me I suppose I must have", or where he admits part only of the ingredients necessary to prove the offence, eg. "I took the car but I thought it must have been abandoned", both the question(s) and the answer(s) must be recorded verbatim. Where an earlier admission is retracted or qualified it will again be necessary to record both question and answer verbatim. Similarly where the accused provides a defence to an allegation going beyond a mere denial of guilt, eg. "When I told you earlier that I stabbed him, what really happened was that I saw the knife on the floor. The man in the red sweater came at me so I picked up the knife and he just sort of ran into it".

Records of Taped Interviews will include marginal notes to indicate the minutes into the interview where admissions or salient points occurred. It is advisable that interviewing officers take notes of relevant times during the interview for retrieval when preparing their Record of Taped Interview in order to avoid the time consuming and unnecessary process of listening to whole interviews.

The amount of verbatim speech included in the Record of Taped Interview will vary with each interview. The objective is to give an account which accurately reflects the content of the interview with the key parts in direct speech. (Officers are reminded that prior to the introduction of contemporaneous notes they summarised interviews by making notes after the interview and attempted to record direct speech as far as it was possible to do so. They are now required to summarise interviews with only the key parts in direct speech and with the help of a tape recording).

The Record of Taped Interview will include the time and date of interview, a note of its duration, the full name of the defendant and the names and rank (where appropriate) of all persons present. Whenever direct speech is referred to in a Record of

Taped Interview the identity of the speaker will be indicated.

When it is necessary for a police officer to submit a statement of evidence reference will be made to the fact that following a taped interview a Record of Taped Interview was prepared and this will be an exhibit produced by the officer preparing the Record of Taped Interview. In cases where two officers are involved in an interview the Record of Taped Interview will be prepared by one officer and one officer only will refer to it in his statement. The second interviewing officer will merely state that he was present at the interview and will make the normal reference to the tape exhibit. Records of Taped Interviews will be entered on a 'Record of Tape Recorded Interview' form (see Appendix).

In cases where a person being interviewed answers 'no comment' or maintains silence throughout the interview there will be no need to prepare a Record of Taped Interview. The fact that the interview took place will be referred to in the officer's statement and reference will be made to the accused remaining silent or consistently answering 'no comment'.

In complicated cases where a series of detailed questions are to be put to a suspect, contemporaneous notes may be used. These will be made whilst the tape is running. In these cases it will not be necessary to prepare a separate Record of Taped Interview. The contemporaneous notes should be submitted to the Crown Prosecution Service.

Divisional/Departmental Commanders will ensure that supervising officers make occasional checks of Records of Taped Interviews and corresponding tapes to ensure consistency in fairness and balance.

ANNEX E: NOTICE TO PERSON WHOSE INTERVIEW HAS BEEN TAPE RECORDED

This notice explains how the tape recording will be used and how you or your solicitor can, if you wish, arrange to listen to it if you are prosecuted.

General

The interview has been recorded on tape. One of these tapes/sets of tapes has been sealed in your presence and will be kept securely in case it is needed in court. The other tape/set of tapes will be a working copy to which the police and you or your solicitor may listen if you wish. Both tapes/sets of tapes are protected against tampering.

[Alternative version if a single deck machine is used:

The interview has been recorded on a tape/set of tapes which is protected against tampering. It has been sealed in your presence and will be kept securely in case it is needed in court. The copy of the tape/set of tapes which was made in your presence will be a working copy to which the police and you or your solicitor may listen if you wish.]

If you have a solicitor
If your solicitor wishes to obtain a copy of the tape he should apply to the Crown Prosecution Service at . . . . . .

If you do not have a solicitor
If you do not have a solicitor now you should think about whether you should seek one. If you do not want a solicitor and you are prosecuted you will, if you wish, be able to listen to the tape recording yourself by applying to the Crown Prosecution Service at . . . . . .

ANNEX F: NOTICE TO SOLICITOR: TAPE RECORDING OF POLICE INTERVIEWS

Name of Defendant:
Tape Reference:
CPS Case Reference:
(*to be quoted in all correspondence*)

1. The enclosed copy of the working copy of . . . . . . tape(s) relate(s) to the interview with your above named client. The copy has/has not been edited to exclude sensitive material as provided for in paragraph 36 of Home Office Circular [/88.]
2. If you wish to take issue with any part of the evidence contained on this recording, or require additional material from the recorded interview to be included in the officer's record of interview you should communicate that fact to the Crown Prosecution Service at the earliest convenient time*. One of the intentions of tape recording is that any dispute arising out of the conduct of the interview or the evidence obtained thereby, be resolved by the defence and prosecution well before the case comes to trial. Thus unnecessary adjournments may be eliminated, together with the risk of consequential awards of costs being ordered against the defendant or his solicitor.

   * The address is:

Index